A CHURCH FOR THE NEXT GENERATION

Sacraments in Transition

Julia Upton, R.S.M.

THE LITURGICAL PRESS
Collegeville, Minnesota

Cover design by David Manahan, O.S.B.

1   2   3   4   5   6   7   8   9

Library of Congress Cataloging-in-Publication Data

Upton, Julia.
    A church for the next generation : sacraments in transition /
Julia Upton.
        p.   cm.
    Includes bibliographical references and index.
    ISBN 0-8146-1952-5
    1. Sacraments—Catholic Church. 2. Catholic Church—Doctrines.
3. Catholic Church—Liturgy. 4. Catholic Church. Ordo initiationis
Christianae adultorum. I. Title.
BX2200.U67 1990
264'.02—dc20   90-42840
                                                          CIP

*For Jeremy and Christian
and their sisters and brothers
around the world—
the Church of the next generation*

Contents

Introduction

In recent years we have witnessed a major shift in the method by which new members are initiated into the Roman Catholic community. Described by Aidan Kavanagh as encompassing a "radical renewal of the whole of Christian life,"[1] the revised Rite of Christian Initiation of Adults [RCIA][2] has been welcomed by those who see in it a liturgical response to the needs of our day, and ignored by those who see in it a complicated public process for what used to be accomplished in private with great alacrity. Whether one has welcomed this rite or has chosen to ignore it, the fact remains that it is dramatically changing the shape of the Church, and knowing the evolutionary process that gave birth to the RCIA will help us to have a better perspective of the Church that is coming to be in the next millennium.

A significant element of the RCIA is the important role given to the worshipping community. In the initiation process, in fact, the Church becomes a ministering community. Each member of the local church community has a clearly defined role in the process, which is surely a dramatic change for those who were raised in the pre-Vatican II Church where participation seemed to be synonymous with passivity. In that era, participation meant following along silently in the missal, standing and kneeling on cue, and never audibly uttering so much as an "Amen." What might appear to be a radical departure from past tradition, however, is more accurately a concept of Church that is firmly grounded in the roots of the Christian story. To know that story is to know the honor of belonging to the ministering community.

With Vatican II the Church entered a new era—an era in which the Church can best be characterized as dynamic, in contrast to the seemingly static Church of the preceding four centuries. When we look to the documents issued by the Second Vatican Council, as well as to the many reforms that were enacted in the two decades following the council, we see precisely how the bishops envisioned the Church of today and tomorrow—as a living, changing organism.[3] Sometimes that vision can be confusing, particularly to people who firmly believed that one of the remarkable qualities of the Church was that it simply could not change. Certainly we know that was never true, but it nevertheless was a misconception that was popularized by the fact that for four hundred years the Church appeared to do little or no changing.[4]

When we return to the historical development of the Church, particularly in its earliest stages, we see patterns of continual growth emerge. Given the pressures and demands of whatever age, we see the Church adapting its theology and ecclesial policy in response, sometimes deliberately, but often accidentally. One dramatic example of this occurred with the "legalization" of Christianity during the reign of Constantine in the fourth century. Prior to that time Christians were not permitted to serve in the army, for it would place them in the untenable position of having to serve two masters—God and the state. Once Christianity was legalized, however, serving in the army actually became the mark of being a good Christian.

It is the purpose of this book to put liturgical change into a historical perspective by focusing on the initiation rite and the effect that our approach to initiation is having on the entire sacramental economy. We will begin by isolating the principles of ecclesial dynamism found in recent ecclesial documents. These set the stage, so to speak, for the unfolding of the drama of change that follows. We will look back into the pages of history to see the important place initiation had in the lives of the Christian people, and the important role each person played in that process of initiation. Then we will look to the present state of initiation into the Roman Catholic community, seeing in it fidelity to the vision of Vatican II as well as to the story of our Christian ancestors. Finally, we will travel to the edge of the future and try to peer into the Church that is coming to be. Given the dynamism of this renewed vision of Church, and the radical change that effects in the community, what might we expect the Church to be like in the future? How would such a Church respond to the problems that face us today?

With the perspective of history, linked to the vision underlying the work of the Second Vatican Council, we should be able to face the future of the ministering community with a confidence rooted in the mystery of death and resurrection, accomplished again and again among Christ's faithful.

NOTES

1. Aidan Kavanagh, "Adult Initiation: Process and Ritual," *Liturgy* 22/1 (1977) 8.

2. In 1974 the International Commission on English in the Liturgy published the English translation of the "provisional" text of the RCIA, which did not have a mandatory date of implementation. The final English translation of the rite was published in 1985, and approved in 1986 by the National Conference of Catholic Bishops at their November meeting. The Rite became mandatory for the diocese of the United States in September of 1988, and will be reviewed again in ten years' time.

3. *See* Hans Kung, *Theology for the Third Millennium: An Ecumenical View* (New York: Doubleday, 1988); Bernard Lee, *The Becoming of the Church: A Process Theology of the Structure of Christian Experience* (New York: Paulist Press, 1974) and *Religious Experience and Process Theology: The Pastoral Implications of a Major Modern Movement*, eds. Harry James Cargas and Bernard Lee (New York: Paulist Press, 1976).

4. A study of the history of the Church during that period of time demonstrates the fallacy of the argument that the Church stood still for four hundred years. However, it is the misunderstanding rather than the reality that directly impacts us.

CHAPTER ONE

Vatican II and Beyond

In the two decades since the conclusion of the Second Vatican Council, as a faith community we have begun to develop a renewed appreciation of our baptismal commitment. Prior to the Council we saw ordination as establishing the only parameters of ministry. That has shifted in the last two decades, and consequently we no longer understand ministry in that limited sense, but as the appropriate response demanded by the commitment that was made by us, or in our name, at baptism. This has altered our concept of both the Church's ministry and its mission in the world, but it was not a change that came about easily or smoothly.

In general there has been an enthusiastic response on the part of the laity to new opportunities in ministry. In 1985 there were 7,204 permanent deacons in the United States, and close to 380,000 Eucharistic ministers. Twenty years ago few people would have even imagined those possibilities. Of course, we all know of those who continue to change lanes during the Communion procession so that they can receive Communion from the priest, but their numbers we hope are gradually diminishing.

The transition, as one might expect, was made more difficult by members of the clergy who believed that allowing members of the laity to share in "their" ministry would cause them to lose status or power. Ironically, we know it is just such an attitude that actually decreases one's power and diminishes one's status.

To understand the shift in the meaning of ministry in the Church, we must look at the Council and what it had to tell us about Church. That will enable us to grasp what is involved in the task of evangelization, and where the need for catechesis lies today.

Defining Church

With Vatican II, as we have noted, came an altered vision of the Church. Prior to that time we viewed Church in terms of a static model—as an institution established in the past and enduring for all times in the same form, with each individual role limited in scope and ministry. In fact, if you will remember, we took great pride in our "unchanging" Church, as well as the confident knowledge that no matter where we traveled in this world, we would be able to "hear" Mass exactly the same as we would in our home parish. This attitude, to say the least, was historically inaccurate, but we had lost a sense of history, probably as far back as the Council of Trent.

The Dogmatic Constitution on the Church issued by Vatican II described a very different Church. Its dominant theme focused upon the Church as the People of God, and in this vision each individual member was to share in the common priesthood of the faithful:

> Though they differ from one another in essence and not only in degree, the common priesthood of the faithful and the ministerial priesthood or hierarchical priesthood are nonetheless interrelated. Each of them in its own special way, is the participation in the one priesthood of Christ. . . . For their part, the faithful join in the offering of the Eucharist by virtue of their royal priesthood. They likewise exercise that priesthood by receiving the sacraments, by prayer and thanksgiving, by witness of a holy life, and by self-denial and active charity.[1]

The constitution is also specific as to the ministerial function of the faithful, who "must assist one another to live holier lives," thus giving the laity "the principal role in the fulfillment of the Church's purpose."[2]

The Council's Decree on the Apostolate of the Laity emphasized the fact that modern conditions necessitate broadening and intensifying this ministerial role.[3] From the text it appears that this viewpoint is a direct result of the recognition that simply by virtue of their life-style lay people are not unable to be ministers of the gospel, as they were often led to believe in the past, but are actually well-equipped for achieving the Church's mission:

> They [the laity] exercise a genuine apostolate by their activity on behalf of bringing the gospel and holiness to all people, and on behalf of penetrating and perfecting the temporal sphere of things through the spirit of the Gospel.[4]

Furthermore, the decree underscores the fact that the laity derive this apostolate from the Lord's command:

Incorporated into Christ's Mystical Body through baptism and strengthened by the power of the Holy Spirit through confirmation, they are assigned to the apostolate by the Lord himself. They are consecrated into a royal priesthood and a holy people (cf. 1 Pet 2:4-10) in order that they may offer spiritual sacrifices through everything they do, and may witness to Christ throughout the world.[5]

AA 3

According to these documents issued by the Second Vatican Council, it is the task of the hierarchy to:

promote the apostolate of the laity, provide it with spiritual principles and support, direct the exercise of this apostolate to the common good of the Church, and attend to the preservation of doctrine and order.[6]

AA 24

The Decree on the Bishops' Pastoral Office in the Church also reminds the bishop that as part of his pastoral function "he should preserve for the faithful the share proper to them in Church affairs; he should also recognize their duty and right to collaborate actively in the building up of the Mystical Body of Christ."[7] At the same time, the Council's Decree on the Church's Missionary Activity encourages the bishops to prepare the laity for this ministry:

Let them train the laity to become conscious of the responsibility which as members of Christ they bear for all people. Let them instruct them deeply in the mystery of Christ, introduce them to practical methods, and be at their side in difficulties, according to the tenor of the Council's Constitution on the Church . . . and its Decree on the Apostolate of the Laity.[8]

AG 21

The same spirit and admonition is also found in the Decree on the Ministry and Life of Priests,[9] for it was the Council's understanding that the laity cooperate in the Church's work of evangelization. "As witnesses and at the same time as living instruments, they share in her saving mission."[10]

In summary, therefore, the Council documents define the Church as the on-going sacrament of God's presence on earth, realized in the community of people who are baptized into the priesthood of the faithful and missioned to the world. Some fulfill their mission in the realm of human affairs, while others do so in the realm of ecclesiastical affairs. All, however, are supported in their corporate mission by the local bishop, whose pastoral function it is to prepare all for ministry.

Evangelization in the Modern World

In 1974 Pope Paul VI convened the fourth international Synod of Bishops for the purpose of discussing evangelization, with the hope that this gathering of bishops would be able to develop some concrete suggestions on evangelization that would enable the Church to stand more boldly in the forefront of contemporary society. At the Synod's conclusion the bishops urged the Pope to make a detailed pronouncement on the subject of evangelization, after studying the working papers of the Synod. Therefore, on December 8, 1975, the Pope issued the Apostolic Exhortation *Evangelii Nuntiandi.*

As do the documents of the Second Vatican Council, this document begins with a specific definition of the Church and its mission:

> The Church is an evangelizer, but she begins by being evangelized herself. She is the community of believers, the community of hope lived and communicated; the community of love; . . . she is the People of God immersed in the world . . . she always needs to be called together afresh by him and reunited. In brief, this means that she wishes to retain freshness, vigor and strength in order to proclaim the Gospel.[11]

Throughout this document, we see that Paul VI recognized evangelization to be the Church's "deepest identity,"[12] and for that reason, in particular, we should never take it lightly, nor as a mere sidelight to being Christian. Rather, evangelization is a duty imposed upon all Christians by command of the Lord Jesus himself, "Go, therefore, make disciples of all nations" (Matt 28:19).

Evangelization involves carrying the good news to all people at every level of society, and in all parts of the world, thereby effecting an inner transformation and renewal, both for those who receive this message, and those who transmit it.[13] The document stresses, furthermore, that evangelization is a complex process which incorporates varied elements—"the renewal of humanity, witness, explicit proclamation, inner adherence, entry into the community, acceptance of signs, and apostolic initiative."[14] If this is to be effective, it must always allow for the "unceasing interplay of the Gospel and of people's concrete lives, both personal and social."[15]

Visions of soap-box preachers dance in our heads, making these recommendations of the Pope seem rather impossible to follow. Surely Paul VI couldn't have meant that we should all go out and preach the good news! Yet, that is exactly what he is trying to emphasize in this document. We must remember, however, that he did understand that there were many levels of evangelization. By looking carefully at the list of elements above, we see many aspects of evangelization that are a normal part of our everyday lives. We need to be aware that these are part of our mission, so that we will enter into them whole-heartedly. For example, one man in our parish is an executive vice-president in a huge multi-national corporation.

There is no doubt in my mind that when he tries to call the corporation to accountability with regard to their involvement in third world countries, he is actively involved in the ministry. Jim exercises a preferential option for the poor in the marketplace, as the Lord Jesus did.

Catechesis and Evangelization: A Necessary Link

We often neglect to consider the effect of the worshipping community on those outside its doors. Too often people make church attendance synonymous with membership. Attendance that is not linked to an appropriate catechesis, however, makes for a stagnant membership and will not result in evangelization, either within the Church or outside its doors. Paul VI referred to this problem specifically:

> It is indeed true that a certain way of administering the sacraments, without the solid support of catechesis, could end up by depriving them of their effectiveness to a great extent. The role of evangelization is precisely to educate people in the faith in such a way as to lead each individual Christian to live the sacraments as true sacraments of faith—and not to receive them passively or to undergo them.[16]

We see here how the areas of catechesis and evangelization are interrelated. Not only does this link give full expression to the sacraments themselves, but it also contributes to the ongoing mission of the community.

In an address made during a general audience on January 12, 1977, Paul VI reiterated his statement that the Church's fundamental mission is spreading the gospel message—a message that is "keenly alive and active in the Church herself."[17] The Pope also identified the present phase in the life of the Church as "an extremely clearly-marked apostolic missionary and didactic phase."[18]

Fundamental to this phase is a proper understanding and appreciation of Christian Initiation:

> its evangelization takes place around the foundation of Christian life which is Baptism, the sacrament of Christian regeneration which must return to being what it was in the conscience and morals of the first Christian generations.[19]

As we shall see in a later chapter, the increasing popularity of infant baptism over the course of time led to a telescoping of the very catechumenal preparation and celebration of which Pope Paul spoke. It was his understanding that our contemporary social environment necessitated a revival of that catechumenal process as a gradual and intensive method of evangelization, in both a pre-baptismal and a post-baptismal context:

in the social environment of today, this method of catechumenate needs to be completed by instruction and by an initiation into the lifestyle characteristic of the Christian, in the period following baptism.[20]

Reflecting this concern, "Catechetics in Our Time" was selected as the theme for the 1977 Synod, which took as its point of reference the evangelical orientation of the previous synod. The 1977 Synod, therefore, sought to examine catechesis within the larger context of the Church.

Catechesis Today

At the conclusion of the International Synod on Catechetics, one group of bishops was charged with the task of summarizing the Synod discussions. Their report contained thirty-four points, and after being amended, the report was sent on to Paul VI. It was also their recommendation that the Pope incorporate their ideas into a magisterial statement on catechesis in the near future.

Paul VI died shortly after the conclusion of the Synod, so the results were not officially presented to the Church until *Catechesi Tradendae* was issued by John Paul II on October 25, 1979. The subject was not neglected in the meantime, however, for both John Paul I and John Paul II had spoken out on the importance of evangelization.[21]

The Synod's report was organized under different headings, the first of which was concerned with the nature of catechesis. The Synod Fathers concurred that "it is necessary to safeguard the harmony between faith and life, to attach sufficient importance to the Sacred Scriptures and to the liturgy, insist on the community nature of existence and offer a clear vision of temporal realities"[22] if catechesis is to be authentic, while avoiding lapse into deviation. Catechesis, therefore, "must be founded upon the faith-experience of the Church and ought to lead one to a gradual deepening of one's faith."[23] In their understanding, "Christian commitment recognizes the concrete necessities of the local Church, and shows itself in a living collaboration in the tasks and activities of the Church."[24]

Once again, from yet another ecclesial body, we identify the now familiar theme that calls for an openness between faith and the world, as well as the need for catechesis to address the exigencies of modern life. Its insistence can hardly be ignored by the leaders of the Church.

In discussing the manner of catechesis, the synodal statement asserted that "catechesis cannot be limited to the task of sacramental preparation, but should continue throughout one's life according to diverse situations and personal and social needs."[25] While recognizing that such a life-long catechesis is vital in today's society, the statement elaborates on the fact that this is not only a Christian's right, but even more importantly it is the Christian's obligation to deepen and mature his or her faith.[26] This is a much more mature approach to catechesis than we have been familiar with in the past. It makes individuals co-responsible for nurturing the life of faith within themselves. In another era we only looked to others to nourish us, but here we see rather clearly that it is always necessary for the Christian to engage in the process of personal faith development.

As the proper context for catechesis, the Synod stressed the Christian community, and urged that:

> In the light of the present situation one should evaluate the initiatives that exist for a catechumenate in preparation for baptism. In the areas of authentic Christian tradition one should seek some form of catechesis which will help the baptizands come to an awareness of their faith, and will help them to live in a coherent way. The question of introducing a catechumenate, in the precise sense, for the baptized, should be carefully studied and experimented with.[27]

Here the suggestion is not to establish a catechumenal process for those who are already baptized. That would, in effect, be tampering with our understanding of the grace that comes with baptism, regardless of the preparation that preceded it. Rather, their suggestion seems to refer to the establishment of a catechumenal community, where one's faith-development would be aided by the presence and experience of others. Unfortunately, by using the word "catechumenal" to refer to people who are baptized, although without benefit of the full experience of the catechumenate that might be desirable, the bishops create a needless confusion. A catechetical community is probably closer to describing what they are suggesting.

The last word of Paul VI on the subject of catechesis came in his closing address to the Synod.[28] The Bishops were exhorted to look to the future, rather than to the past, and to appeal "to all those who feel their responsibility as Christians" to dedicate themselves to renew their catechetical mission.[29] Toward this end, the Pope was pleased by the unanimity exhibited in the discussions on the content of catechesis, agreeing with the bishops that the systematic character of catechesis is absolutely necessary for an orderly study of the Christian mystery, and forms the basis for distinguishing catechesis from all other proclamations of the Word of God.[30]

In his Apostolic Exhortation *Catechesi Tradendae*, John Paul II linked evangelization and catechesis, and encouraged that both be adapted to the life and needs of those being taught or evangelized.[31] Linking catechesis to the whole of liturgical and sacramental activity, he used the catechumenate as a model:

> In the early Church, the catechumenate and preparation for the sacraments of baptism and the Eucharist were the same thing. Although in the countries that have long been Christian the Church has changed her practice in this field, the catechumenate has never been abolished; on the contrary, it is experiencing a renewal in those countries and is abundantly practiced in the young missionary churches.[32]

He warned, however, that catechesis will only thrive in a community of faith, and will otherwise stagnate:

> the ecclesial community at all levels has a two-fold responsibility with regard to catechesis: it has the responsibility of providing for the training of its members, but it also has the responsibility of welcoming them into an environment where they can live as fully as possible what they have learned.[33]

Following the 1987 Synod of Bishops which studied the vocation and mission of the laity in the Church, John Paul II issued the Apostolic Exhortation *Christifideles Laici*.[34] In this document the Pope again made it clear that the laity, together with the clergy, are responsible for the mission of the Church, specifically in proclaiming the Gospel.[35] To this end the Pope proposed that what is needed at the present moment is a process of what he terms "re-evangelization," which will result in the "formation of mature ecclesial communities, in which the faith might radiate and fulfill the basic meaning of adherence to the person of Christ and his Gospel, of an encounter and sacramental communion with him, and of an existence lived in charity and in service."[36] The effect the RCIA is having on our sacramental economy, as we shall see in the chapters that follow, will help to lead us toward the goal of this papal mandate.

By examining these official ecclesiastical pronouncements, therefore, it has become increasingly evident that the Magisterium is rather insistent in its belief that all members of the Christian community must share in the task of evangelization, so that Christ's command may be fulfilled. They must recognize their personal obligation of intensifying their own faith-commitment, and must testify by their everyday lives that "Jesus Christ is Lord!" These are not the tasks of a static Church, but of a dynamic Church that is on pilgrimage to its fulfillment in the kingdom of heaven.

NOTES

1. Dogmatic Constitution on the Church *(Lumen Gentium [LG])* no. 10 in *The Documents of Vatican II,* ed. Walter M. Abbott (New York: American Press, 1966), 27. All further references to conciliar documents are to this text.

2. *LG,* no. 36, 63.

3. Decree on the Apostolate of the Laity *(Apostolicam Actuositatem [AA])* no. 1, 490.

4. *AA,* no. 2, 491.

5. *AA,* no. 3, 492.

6. *AA,* no. 24, 513.

7. Decree on the Bishops' Pastoral Office in the Church *(Christus Dominus [CD])* no. 16, 409.

8. Decree on the Church's Missionary Activity *(Ad Gentes [AG])* no. 21, 612.

9. See Decree on the Ministry and Life of Priests *(Presbyterorum Oridinis [PO])* no. 9, 553.

10. *AG,* no. 41, 628.

11. Paul VI, *Evangelii Nuntiandi [EN]* (Washington: United States Catholic Conference, 1976) no. 15, 13–14.

12. *EN,* no. 14, 12.

13. *EN,* no. 18, 15.

14. *EN,* no. 24, 19.

15. *EN,* no. 29, 22.

16. *EN,* no. 47, 32.

17. As reported in *L'Osservatore Romano,* (January 13, 1977) 1–2. In attendance were numerous members of "neo-catechumenate communities."

18. *Ibid.* 1.

19. *Ibid.*

20. *Ibid.*

21. John Paul I addressed the bishops of the Philippines on the subject during their *ad limina* visit on September 28, 1978, and John Paul II spoke about the necessity of evangelization to the bishops of New Zealand during their *ad limina* visit on November 13, 1978.

22. *L'Osservatore Romano,* (November 17, 1977) 6. [All further references to the summary statement issued by the 1977 Synod are to this text.]

23. *Ibid.*

24. *Ibid.*

25. *Ibid.*

26. *Ibid.*

27. *Ibid.* 7.

28. *See* Paul VI, "Closing Address," *The Living Light* 15 (1978) 98–100.

29. *Ibid.* 99.

30. *Ibid.* 100.

31. John Paul II, *Catechesi Tradendae [CT]* no. 18, *Origins* 9 (1979) 334.

32. *CT,* no. 23, 335.

33. *CT,* no. 24, 336.

34. This post-synodal document [CL] was issued on December 30, 1988, and was published in *Origins* 18 (1989) 561–95.

35. *CL,* no. 33.

36. *CL,* no. 34.

CHAPTER TWO

Missioned to the World

As Catholic Christians, we are not only moved and shaped by the environment within the Church, but we are also affected by the world outside the Church. We recall that recently a group of musicians raised millions of dollars to help relieve the famine in Ethiopia by reminding us of the simple fact that "we *are* the world." That brings back to consciousness the old biblical imperative that Christians must live *in* the world, without being *of* the world—without allowing themselves to be co-opted by a value system that is alien to the teachings of Jesus. Companies might sometimes have us believe that it is perfectly all right to step on other people as we climb our way to the top. Advertisers might have us believe that material things will bring us happiness, and mouthwash will bring us love. The list could go on and on, reminding all Christians that until we enter the heavenly Jerusalem we will continue to live and work in an alien land.

When confronted by the world of his day, William Wordsworth responded in these words:

> The world is too much with us; late and soon,
> Getting and spending, we lay waste our powers:
> Little we see in Nature that is ours;
> We have given our hearts away, a sordid boon!
> This Sea bares her bosom to the moon;
> The winds that will be howling at all hours,
> And are up-gathered now like sleeping flowers;
> For this, for everything, we are out of tune;
> It moves us not. —Great God! I'd rather be
> A Pagan suckled in a creed outworn;
> So might I, standing on this pleasant lea,
> Have glimpses that would make me less forlorn;

Have sight of Proteus rising from the sea;
Or hear old Triton blow his wreathed horn.[1]

That was his response to the world he knew—the oppressive, pre-industrialized London society of 1806. When you think of how far technology has progressed in the intervening centuries, you wonder what would he ever have to say about our world today!

Because we do live on foreign soil, so to speak, the world continues to pose a challenge to Christians on many different levels. Science requires us to approach each new discovery with eyes and minds open to wonder. Philosophy asks us to find new ways of articulating the principles that underlie the human enterprise. Sociology calls us to question whether we value community more than autonomy. History demands that we look at the past objectively, for it can be our wisest teacher. How, then, shall we respond as Christians when we are confronted by the many facets of our world?

The Scientific Focus

Since the advent of the atomic age, scientific knowledge has increased in astronomical proportions. Yesterday's science fiction has become today's scientific fact, with a rapidity that can scarcely be charted. Similarly, tomorrow's science fiction cannot even be imagined! The extra-terrestrial exploration that occupied the headlines so recently has now taken its place on the back pages, giving way to intra-cellular exploration. No longer does the nation stop to watch in awe at the launch pad. Yesterday's awe has settled into ordinariness and become commonplace fare.

Once upon a time, people thought that they lived in a relatively stable world. They lived one or two generations while nothing very significant in the world surrounding them changed. Fashion, transportation, communication—everything moved slowly. Our experience is vastly different, however, and consequently we know now that neither the universe nor the laws which govern it are static or clearly defined; rather they are dynamic and continually open for revision. "We always did it that way" is no longer defensible. With every new venture into the world of science, some age-old belief seems to be challenged.

Actually the world of science has influenced the world of philosophy. As citizens of a scientifically-oriented, space-age society, we know that our universe is alive, with all of its various material elements in perpetual motion. The fact that Stephen Hawking's masterpiece *A Brief History of Time: From the Big Bang to Black Holes* has topped the non-fiction best-seller charts since its publication witnesses to the dramatic encounter between science and philosophy.

Hawking writes for a general audience without pre-supposing them to have a scientific education, presenting what he terms "basic ideas" about the origin and fate of the universe. His questions ask "What do we know about the universe, and how do we know it? Where did the universe come from, and where is it going? Did the universe have a beginning, and if so, what happened before then? What is the nature of time? Will it ever come to an end?"[2] We know these questions to be familiar. They have been asked over and over again by philosophers and scientists alike since ancient times. Their answers, as Hawking notes, may neither affect our life-style nor aid the survival of our species, but this fundamental human yearning is reason enough to continue the quest.[3]

The Social Perspective

Just as the 1960s were characterized by an anti-establishment revolt against the unpopular manipulation of peoples' lives which resulted from our country's involvement in the war in Southeast Asia, so the 1970s witnessed a similar anti-establishment shift. In that decade, however, the shift was of a more spiritual nature. The so-called spiritual revolution that arose in the late 1970s seemed to be a reaction to society's materialism—a materialism that resulted in a depersonalized, mechanized society.

The pervasive movement of the new revolution, one could say, is more toward isolating and celebrating that which is basic to humanity and which unites all people. This occurs in a wide variety of patterns, sparked by many different approaches, both within and outside the Church. Familiar examples of this trend include Marriage Encounter, the Charismatic Renewal, as well as Rev. Sun Myung Moon's Unification Church.

And what has been happening in the 1980s? Actually, the fads of the 1970s have either vanished or settled into the patterns of establishment. Ironically, as we move into the closing decade of the twentieth century, establishment is in vogue in many circles, which lends a helping-hand of credibility to those spiritual movements that were once scoffed at for being too much on the fringe of society to be taken seriously.

At St. Martin's in 1976, people cast a suspicious eye at those charismatics who gathered every Tuesday in the Hogans' basement for a prayer meeting. All sorts of bizarre rumors spread about what they were doing— speaking in tongues, being baptized and slain in the Spirit, etc. Participants were automatically labeled as weird. Thirteen years later, the same group meets on Tuesday evenings, but now they meet in the church. The former weirdos are respected members of the community, active also as lectors and Eucharistic ministers, and even serve as members of the parish council.

It could be that such groups have served as catalysts for change, helping to develop in us a deeper sense of community.

Calling for Action

The leaders of the Roman Catholic Church in the United States attempted to respond in a positive manner to Vatican II's challenge to develop a means for the direct participation of the faithful in ecclesial administration. Their most significant step in that direction, aside from including lay advisors on the various committees that form the working mechanism of the National Council of Catholic Bishops, was the "Call to Action."[4] The culmination of a two-year series of regional, diocesan, and parish hearings, this conference was attended by 1300 delegates united by the common purpose of establishing U.S. Catholic social priorities for the following five years.

In inaugurating this process of consultation in February of 1975, Cardinal John Dearden expressed the purpose of the "Call to Action":

> our goal should be to awaken a new vision and sense of purpose in our community, to develop forms of Christian work and ministry appropriate to these new-found purposes and appropriate to the scope and depth of the problems we face.[5]

Although the conference considered many specific subjects, organized under broader headings,[6] its concerns for the Christian community itself were considered in the context of "personhood." These statements followed from the basic tenet that "the universal Church proclaims that faith in Jesus Christ as Lord and mutual care for persons foster the common life of the community and affirm the dignity of each Christian."[7] In this context they urged:

1. Development of a sense of community, particularly at the parish level.
2. An increased awareness of the fact that each person has a personal Christian vocation which should be recognized and nurtured in a creative and receptive environment.
3. Recognition that individual gifts should be used for the benefit of all.
4. Creation of different environments (parochial, diocesan, familial) in which all people can respond to the universal call to holiness.[8]

In a speech delivered to the Bavarian Catholic Academy in Munich, West Germany, on November 30, 1976, Msgr. George Higgins underscored

the importance of the Call to Action as the first evidence of "shared responsibility" in the ecclesial system. As such he believed it should be evalu-
ated "as part of an on-going process whereby the various sectors of the
Catholic community in the United States are brought into closer collaboration and cooperation with the hierarchy and with one another on all
matters affecting the life of the Church."[9] In this light the Call to Action
can be seen as the first conference which gave a major thrust toward actualizing the post-Vatican II need for shared responsibility. As such it was
only the beginning of a process that we have seen continuing under the
sponsorship of various groups.[10]

In a variety of contexts, ecclesiastical declarations in the post-Vatican II
era have repeatedly reaffirmed a vision of the Church as a dynamic organism in which each member's active participation is essential to the life
of the Church. Liberation theologians, for example, give voice to the dynamism of the Church, for they see the mission of the Church not in the
static model of being the deposit of faith, but in the vibrant model as being the servant of all people.[11]

All of us share in the task of evangelization and are challenged continually to renew and deepen our personal faith-commitment. Where this
message has been transmitted it has been met with a positive response
from the People of God, who are anxious and pre-disposed by their experience in the world outside the Church to view themselves as playing
an active role in governing the Church, as with their fellow pilgrims they
journey through this life. The response, however, is of limited dimension,
for it comes from only a narrow segment of the faithful—those who have
been made aware of this ecclesial vision and have been given a direction
or a model into which they can channel their response.

The greater majority of the faithful, however, have not viewed themselves either as necessary members of the Church, or as active participants
in its operation. Instead they still conceive of themselves merely as pas-
sive recipients of ecclesiastical services.[12] At the present moment, therefore, the task of evangelization must encompass not only doctrinal data,
but also an authentic understanding of what it means to be a Church as
well as an appreciation of the various roles which all members of the community play within the Church.

The Historical View

In the olden days, history was one thing we were certain could never
change. After all, the past was over and done with. How could that pos-
sibly change?

Although history doesn't change, our reading of it can and does change
from century to century. We take into consideration the limitations of
writers and the influences present in the era in which they lived and wrote.
The result is that history appears to change, when in actuality all that
has been provided is a more accurate presentation of history.

History shows us that the Church we were once so sure was magically
preserved from change has certainly grown and changed throughout its
history. Our focus in this book is on the impact present practice of initiation into the Christian community (RCIA) is having on the rest of our
sacramental economy. An accurate reading of the history of initiation practice, therefore, will be indispensible to our understanding and appreciation of this impact.

The New Testament does not give us a complete picture of initiation
practices in the early Church. Rather than being a historical document
in itself, the New Testament is a compilation of different types of
writings—the Gospels, the Letters, the Acts of the Apostles, and
Revelation—none of which was specifically intended to be a history of
the Church. It is not surprising, therefore, that in studying the history
of initiation practice, the New Testament is of value only indirectly.

By the fourth century, we find an availability of historical documents
that speak specifically of initiation practice. We have, for example, collections of homilies that were intended for audiences of catechumens, which
help us to establish a fairly accurate picture of initiation practices at that
time.

The Apostolic Era

With the knowledge of those later practices, when we look back to the
New Testament we are able to hypothesize about initiation in the earliest
days of the Church. This is possible when we examine the metaphorical
language employed by the writers of the New Testament in the light of
what we know to be later practice. Such evidence is clearly circumstan-
tial, and surely would never stand up in a court of law, but it is the best
that we can manage to piece together. A few examples will help to illus-
trate the importance of examining historical data in this context.

In the fourth century, it is apparent from the texts that a special relationship was established between catechumens, their sponsors, and their
instructors. We can deduce from the writings of St. Paul, three hundred
years earlier, that there might also have been a special relationship between the instructor and the individual called to faith: "People under in-

struction should always contribute something to the support of the person who is instructing them" (Gal 6:6).

We know that in the fourth century it was common practice to baptize people by immersion. Given the following metaphor, it is also possible that the early Church practiced baptism by immersion as well, when we read "when we were baptized we went into the tomb with him and joined him in death, so that as Christ was raised from the dead by the Father's glory, we too might live a new life" (Rom 6:1).

While later documents clearly state that the newly baptized person wore a special garment to symbolize his or her new life, this might also have been practiced in the New Testament churches, as alluded to in the following metaphor: "All baptized in Christ, you have all clothed yourselves in Christ" (Gal 3:27).

It is also possible that the New Testament churches anointed the newly baptized, as did churches in the fourth century, for St. Paul also writes, "you too have been stamped with the seal of the Holy Spirit of the Promise" (Eph 1:13).

Perhaps the lack of direct New Testament evidence is not only due to a reluctance to commit anything incriminating to writing during an era of persecution, but also to a lack of standard practice. It could very well be that Paul's ritual of initiation differed substantially from James', but there is no evidence of that either. It is just one of my liturgical hunches.

A Growing Church

As the Church expanded, however, the need for a standardization of catechetical instruction became more acute. In both the *Didache* (c. 140) and the Epistle of Barnabas (c. 100) we find what Church historians refer to as the "two-way" material. It is a primitive form of religious instruction, which is presented as two different ways in which one can choose to live: the way of light or the way of darkness. While both documents contain essentially the same material, indicating a similar source, neither gives us any information as to how the catechetical process occurred.

It is not until the *Apostolic Tradition* of Hippolytus (c. 215), in fact, that a highly developed rite of initiation, replete with a serious catechumenate, is described. We have evidence for the first time, for example, that not everyone was eligible for acceptance into the Christian communities, indicating that the communities themselves were becoming very selective. What might appear to us as stringent requirements had been set down governing those who wished to be considered for candidacy.

Unless the individual met those standards, he or she could not pursue Christian training.[13] These precautions, we suspect, were taken in part to guard against pagan infiltration, not to make Christian communities elitist groups.

Persons seeking admission into the community first of all had to be *Sponsor* introduced to the teachers by a reputable member of the community. Thorough questioning of the candidates was intended to reveal their modes of life, as well as the integrity of their intentions to become Christians. Certain occupations were considered to be incompatible with the Christian vocation, so unless the candidates were willing to forsake their suspect professions, they would be barred from gaining entrance into the catechumenate. Such occupations would naturally include brothel-keepers and prostitutes; but sculptors, teachers, actors, gladiators, and soldiers were also considered suspect, because of the nature of those occupations at that time.[14] To be a soldier, for example, would require a dual loyalty— to God and to the emperor—which Christianity did not allow at that time. Similarly, teachers in that era were proponents of pagan philosophy, which was considered to be incompatible with Christianity.

Upon being accepted by the teachers, the candidates were enrolled in the Order of Catechumens in a public ceremony. Ordinarily the catechumenate was of three years' duration, during which time the catechumens were thoroughly instructed in doctrinal, moral, and ascetical principles. Catechumens were permitted to attend community services, but they were required to leave for special instructions during the celebration of the Eucharist.[15]

On the first Sunday of the Lent preceding their baptism, the catechumens entered a special period of preparation as *illuminandi*.[16] The culmination of this final preparatory stage occurred at the Easter Vigil when the catechumens were baptized and sealed with the Spirit, and shared fully in the Eucharistic celebration for the first time.[17]

After the persecutions came to an end and greater numbers of people began to be converted to Christianity, the catechumenate was a powerful element in the life of church communities because it actually involved the entire community in the process of initiation. Once Christianity became the official religion of the Roman Empire at the end of the fourth century, however, it became increasingly impossible to retain the former structure of the catechumenate.

Communities no longer needed to fear pagan infiltration, and consequently were less suspicious of people who wanted to become Christians. Candidates' motives, therefore, were not so scrupulously examined, and as a result not all had pure motives for becoming catechumens. Because catechumens were entitled to all of the benefits of belonging to the Christian community—with the exception of participation in the Eucharist—without having to undergo any of its rigors, many individuals were satisfied with remaining indefinitely in the order of Catechumens.[18] To become a baptized Christian, for example, meant one took on the obligation of obeying all of the laws of the Church. Penance, we recall, was long and public in those days, so by remaining a catechumen one had the prestige of membership without all of the obligations that accompanied it. For example, one could continue to sin as much as one pleased, knowing that baptism would wash away all sin, without the humiliation of penance.

The Middle Ages witnessed the complete demise of adult initiation into the Christian community, resulting primarily from what had become the more common procedure of initiation—infant baptism. This, of course, did not happen overnight. The triumph of Christianity over paganism meant that fewer adults were seeking entrance into the community. Augustine's teaching on original sin made the practice of early baptism emotionally, if not theologically, mandatory.[19] Therefore, by the seventh century the majority of people were received into the community as infants.

The gradual growth and eventual demise of the ritualization of initiation into the Christian community gives dramatic testimony to the relationship between God and God's people throughout these centuries. Initially faith was seen as a total commitment of one's life to God and to the community. The more seriously this faith-commitment was taken, the more thorough were the instructions. Similarly, the initiation ceremony itself was quite elaborate, and was carried out with great jubilation.

With the high mortality rate resulting from the Black Death and numerous wars and political rebellions, it is not surprising for us to see that attention came to be focused on death rather than on life. This, coupled with the Church's emphasis on original sin, had a devastating effect on community life. People's whole relationship with God and each other was muted. What had formerly been cause for intensive training and jubilant celebration devolved into a private practice of lustration, the result of an overriding fear of eternal damnation. The concept of community in relation to initiation, in particular, was literally destroyed, and replaced with an individualization of religious practice unknown and alien to the concept of Christianity developed in the days of the first followers of Jesus.

In Summary

Having taken a brief look at the pressures exerted on the Church from some of the various worlds that form our environment, we see the necessity for having a developmental ecclesiology. It is unrealistic for us to postulate a principle that the Church is immutable. All living organisms grow and change, literally making change an attribute of life. Such a vision is not a radical departure from the Church before Vatican II; it is a natural part of realizing that we are the Church.

Difficulty, however, seems to arise from a realization that the consequent concept of shared responsibility is not being adequately addressed or practiced by those who are in a position to do so. What is needed at the present time is a model to demonstrate to both clergy and laity the positive results of actualizing a developmental ecclesiology. This will be accomplished in succeeding chapters.

NOTES

1. *The Mentor Book of Major Poets*, ed. Oscar Williams (New York: The New American Library, 1963) 68.

2. Stephen W. Hawking, *A Brief History of Time: From the Big Bang to Black Holes* (New York: Bantam Books, 1988) 1.

3. *Ibid.* 13.

4. Intended to be part of the U.S. Catholic Church's observance of the nation's bicentennial, this conference was held in Detroit, October 21-23, 1976. A good synthesis of the work of this conference may be found in Frank Manning's work *A Call to Action: An Interpretive Summary and Guide* (Notre Dame: Fides, 1977), although a more complete documentary study is found in *A Call to Action: An Agenda for the Catholic Community* (Washington: United States Catholic Conference, 1977).

5. Cardinal John Dearden, "Awakening a New Vision," *Origins* 4 (1975) 548.

6. These broader categories were: Church, family, neighborhood, work, ethnicity and race, personhood, nationhood, and humankind.

7. "Personhood: Justice Conference Resolutions," *Origins* 6 (1976) 314.

8. *Ibid.* 314-17.

9. "Beyond Religious Freedom: Church in Society," *Origins* 6 (1976) 404.

10. "Shared responsibility" has been attempted on both the parochial and diocesan levels. On the whole, however, parish councils and diocesan pastoral councils have failed to effect genuine dialogue, and more often are merely caricatures of what was originally intended by their formation. Cf. Bishop H. Hubbard, "Shared Responsibility in the Local Church," *Origins* 8 (1979) 615-24; Bishop A. Attenweller, "Parish Renewal, A Process Not a Program," *Origins* 8 (1979) 672-76, C. Campbell, "The Parish Council Syndrome," *Homiletic and Pastoral Review* 79 (1979) 40-54.

11. Gustavo Gutierrez, *A Theology of Liberation: History, Politics and Salvation* (Maryknoll: Orbis, 1973) 256. *See also* Leonardo Boff, *Ecclesiogenesis: The Base Communities Reinvent the Church* (Maryknoll: Orbis, 1986).

12. *See The Notre Dame Study of Catholic Parish Life* (South Bend: Notre Dame University Press, 1987); *Religion in America* (Chicago: Thomas More Press, 1976) 89–102; *Faith and Ferment: An Interdisciplinary Study of Christian Beliefs and Practices*, ed. Joan D. Chittister and Martin Marty (Minneapolis: Augsburg, 1983); Michael Warren, *Faith, Culture and the Worshipping Community: Shaping the Practice of the Local Church* (New York: Paulist Press, 1989).

13. *Apostolic Tradition of St. Hippolytus* [*AT*] no. 15, ed. Gregory Dix (London: SPCK, 1968) 15.

14. *AT*, no. 16, 15–16.

15. *AT*, no. 18, 16–17.

16. This descriptive term was native to the East. In Rome they were traditionally known as *electi*, while in other areas of the West they were referred to as *competentes*.

17. *AT*, no. 21, 18–22.

18. See Nathan D. Mitchell, "Dissolution of the Rite of Christian Initiation," in *Made Not Born: New Perspectives on Christian Initiation and the Catechumenate* (Notre Dame: University of Notre Dame Press, 1976) 50–75.

19. Augustine, *City of God*, Book XIII, Chapter 14 (Garden City: Doubleday, 1958) 278–79.

CHAPTER THREE

Christian Initiation Today

The RCIA, as it is referred to in current liturgical jargon, did not just appear one day on the Pope's desk. Its gestation was in itself an interesting story of how sacramental practice evolves in the twentieth century.

Prior to the first publication of the *Rite of Christian Initiation of Adults* [RCIA] in 1974,[1] the Ritual of Pope Paul V (1614) was the official ritual of baptism. Published as a result of the decision of the Council of Trent (1545–63), this ritual simply codified what had become common practice in the eighth century, without any attempt to distinguish between adult baptism and infant baptism.

In the sixth and seventh centuries, adult initiation came to be less common, taking the back seat to infant baptism. The *Ordo Romanus* XI (700–750) reflected that change. For symbolical reasons, one would conclude, the pre-baptismal rites were divided into seven sections, known as *scrutinia*. Except for the name, these bore nothing in common with the scrutinies as we use the term today when speaking of initiation into the Christian community. Rather than critical examinations, they were simple pieces of a ritual derived from the *Gelasian Sacramentary* (sixth century), and severely compressed, as you can plainly see. They included:

1. Imposition of name, basic catechesis, act of aversion from error and conversion to God, first solemn signing.
2. Ceremony of tasting salt.
3–5. Solemn exorcisms (repeated three times).
6. Solemn entrance, bestowal of the Creed and the Lord's prayer, final exorcism, the rite of opening the ears, anointing with the oil of catechumens after the renunciation of Satan.
7. Baptism.

Obviously, this was one part of the Roman Ritual that needed serious attention, not only to distinguish between adult and infant candidates, but also to insure that the practice of initiation was consonant with the ecclesiology professed and practiced.

Origins of the RCIA

As the liturgical movement gained impetus in the decades preceding Vatican II, pressure was continually exerted on the Sacred Congregation of Rites to initiate some type of reform of the baptismal ritual.[2] This pressure came from two directions: liturgical scholars were anxious to implement a rite which would be more in line with the principles and practices of the early Church, while bishops of mission countries found that the catechumenal model provided more adequately for the needs of their communities, and were therefore insistent on the development of a ritual which would incorporate that model. What both of these groups were seeking, it would seem, was a longer period of initiation accompanied by suitable intermediary rites.

In response to these various demands, the Sacred Congregation of Rites issued a decree on April 16, 1962, which allowed for the division of the ritual then in use into seven separate and distinct stages.[3] By this means the Sacred Congregation hoped to solve two problems: to deter the introduction of unsuitable variations of the rite which individuals might develop; and to eliminate the deficiencies of the Ordo of 1614. In effect, one can say that this alteration constituted official sanction for the revival of the catechumenate, in principle, because it resulted in a model of initiation in stages. This attempt at reform failed, however, to achieve either of its purposes, which becomes evident after an examination of the significant amount of literature it occasioned.[4]

The ritual itself, as we saw earlier, was little more than a conglomeration of disjointed rites. Simply to separate these steps, therefore, did nothing to make them flow as coherent elements of a single process of initiation. The division was thus rejected as unacceptable throughout the world. In the United States, the episcopal conference requested and was granted an indult which allowed priests to continue to baptize adults using the ritual they used for the baptism of infants.

Complete revision of the baptismal ritual was to become a reality only after Vatican II. Such a program was mandated by the Fathers of the Second Vatican Council, as expressed in The Constitution on the Sacred Liturgy:

> The catechumenate for adults, comprising several distinct steps, is to be restored and to be put into use at the discretion of the local ordinary.

By this means the period of the catechumenate, which is intended as a time of suitable instruction, may be sanctified by sacred rites to be celebrated at successive intervals.[5]

Both of the rites for the baptism of adults are to be revised: not only the simpler rite, but also the more solemn one, which must take into account the restored catechumenate.[6]

From this we can see that the restoration of the catechumenate was envisioned as a concept separate from the formulation of a new rite, and consequently was thus not dependent on the rite for implementation. Furthermore, the gravity with which the Council fathers viewed this ritual reform and its fulcrum—the re-establishment of the catechumenate—is also evidenced by the fact that this subject of Christian initiation, with its resultant impact on the community, was also discussed in several other conciliar documents.[7]

Implementing Reform

The machinery for implementing the liturgical reforms ordered by Vatican II was announced by Paul VI on January 25, 1964, in the *motu proprio, Sacram Liturgicam:*

> It is clear that many prescriptions of the Constitution cannot be effected within a short span since the various rites must be revised thoroughly and the liturgical books carefully worked on. So that this task may go forward with the wisdom and courageous balance required, we establish a special commission the chief obligation of which will be to bring to completion the matters prescribed in the Constitution on the Liturgy.[8]

In keeping with the program established in that document, on February 29, 1964, the *Consilium ad Exsequendum Constitutionem de Sacra Liturgia*[9] was organized, comprising approximately fifty episcopal members and over 200 consultors. The *Consilium*, in turn, charged a commission of twelve members [*Coetus* 22][10] with the task of formulating rites for the restoration of the catechumenate, and the baptism of both adults and infants [CSL 64–70].

Specific guidelines were approved by the episcopal members of the *Consilium* at its first plenary session in the fall of 1964. These were intended to give direction to the commissions [22 and 23] charged with the revision of the Roman Ritual, and indicated that their work should:

1. Clearly express that the rites encourage the active participation of the faithful in the mysteries of salvation.

2. Research traditional elements used in the catechumenate to insure continuity between the ancient forms and the new forms.
3. Show the connection between the action of God signified through the rites, and the catechumen's progress toward baptism.
4. Eliminate whatever does not correspond to the modern mentality or situation.
5. Give episcopal conferences latitude to adapt the rites to local needs, especially in mission countries.[11]

When *Coetus* 22 met for the first time in September of 1964, the members drafted a general outline for revision of the ritual of adult baptism. They envisioned formulating two rituals—a solemn one, and a more simple ritual. In developing the solemn ritual their plan was:

1. To express in liturgical language a rite for each step in the initiation process.
2. To insert readings from sacred scripture.
3. To develop a series of prayers and exorcisms so that the catechumenal progress to baptism is clear and apparent.
4. To allow episcopal conferences to omit a few or all of these rites, after taking persons and places into consideration.
5. To urge that baptism take place in the presence of the faithful at the Easter Vigil.
6. To allow priests who baptize adults the faculty to confirm them as well, so that the initiation process could be complete.[12]

In the simple ritual they wanted to maintain the traditional schema, and to emphasize three significant moments:

1. Introduction into the catechumenate.
2. *Traditio symboli.*
3. Sacramental washing.[13]

These ideas were fleshed out in meetings held throughout that winter.

Evolution of a Ritual

Using the 1962 reform of the Rite of Baptism in the Roman Ritual as the foundation, the *Coetus* sought to incorporate both ancient and modern sources of liturgical tradition into their revision, which necessitated an examination of oriental liturgies as well as those of other Christian communities. On the pastoral level, the work being carried out in the catechumenal centers of France[14] and various mission countries was recognized to be of great value, and was therefore an important element in the

Coetus' study. A report of *Coetus* 22, and a series of questions[15] were submitted to the *Consilium* for consideration at its meeting in April of 1965.

Having gained the approval of the *Consilium, Coetus* 22 then moved on to developing the first draft of the *Ordo Initiationis Christianae Adultorum* [OICA], which was submitted to the *Consilium* at its October 1965 meeting. The draft divided the initiation process into four steps:

1. Entrance into the catechumenate: including such rites as imposition of hands and signing of the forehead. It also provided minor exorcisms to be celebrated during the catechumenate, and prayers and blessings for the catechumens.
2. Election: inscription of names.
3. Scrutinies and Traditions.
4. Rite of Immediate Preparation/Sacraments of Initiation.[16]

A few minor changes were recommended at that time, and these were incorporated into the second draft (March 18, 1966), which was sent to fifty catechumenal centers, located in various parts of the world, for the purpose of experimentation. For that reason, this particular draft, *Schemata* 147/*De Rituali* 9, included not only the experimental ritual, but also an Appendix which contained supplementary material to aid the process of experimentation. The *Coetus* also planned to include a *Praenotanda*, but it was not included in this draft. These additions included some explanatory notes, guidelines for conducting the experiment, and a specific format for reporting to the *Consilium* the results of the experiment.

The evaluations submitted by the experimental centers[17] were collated and circulated among the members of *Coetus* 22 prior to their meeting at Vanves, France, (December 30, 1968, to January 4, 1969) where the results were discussed.[18] Since *Schemata* 147/*De Rituali* 9 did not include the projected *Praenotanda*, the questionaires revealed many difficulties which could have been eliminated. For example, the evaluations reflected concern for incorporating models for possible adaptation, and confusion on the importance of different elements of the ritual, some of which were considered to be antiquated and incompatible with the ecumenical spirit found in the Church at that time. The pastoral concern which these conclusions manifest is for a clear, concise, liturgical celebration not bogged down with meaningless, time-consuming incoherencies. The *Coetus* found these criticisms valuable and they formed the basis for the revised text and the formulations of the *Praenotanda*.

Therefore, a new draft (*Schemata* 344/*De Rituali* 35) was prepared. This draft included the *Praenotandu* and was dated June 21, 1969. Further refinements were made during the summer, and the final draft (*Schemata* 352/*De Rituali* 36) was prepared for the Fall meeting of the *Consilium*, where it was approved. After being circulated among the various Roman congregations, the OICA was finally published by the Congregation for Divine Worship on January 6, 1972.[19]

Structure of the RCIA

Liturgical documents can be critically examined from many different perspectives, but since our purpose here is to demonstrate that this particular document presupposes a developmental vision of the Church, it will be helpful to analyze the RCIA canonically, ritually, and catechetically.

Canonical Analysis

Canonically, the catechumenate is a juridical organization which corresponds to the entire length of initiation. Adults asking to be baptized are admitted to the catechumenate and led through several stages to sacramental initiation.[20] Within this structure there are four distinct stages:

a. The *pre-catechumenate* refers to the initial period of evangelization, suited to the individual needs of those who show an interest in becoming members of the community. The nature of this stage, therefore, requires a flexible structure of indeterminate length. Beginning with the first preaching of the gospel, this is a special time of inquiry which reaches its culmination in the individual's informed decision to pursue the catechetical and ritual process of becoming a Christian.

> From evangelization, completed with the help of God, come the faith and initial conversion that cause a person to feel called away from sin and drawn toward the mystery of God's love. The whole period of the pre-catechumenate is set aside for this evangelization, so that the genuine will to follow Christ and seek baptism may mature.[21]

b. The *catechumenate* is generally the longest of these periods, encompassing the entire span of catechetical preparation. It is suggested in the *Praenotanda* that this period should span several years, during which time the clergy, catechists, godparents and/or sponsors, and other interested members of the community join in the conversion process.

> From this time on the Church embraces the catechumens as its own with a mother's love and concern. Joined to the Church, the catechumens are now part of the household of Christ, since the Church nourishes them with

the word of God and sustains them by means of liturgical celebrations. The catechumens should be eager, then, to take part in celebrations of the word of God and to receive blessings and other sacramentals.[22]

c. The *period of purification and enlightenment*, corresponding to the season of Lent, is the time set aside for more profound preparation, rooted more in spiritual than in catechetical development.

d. The *mystagogical phase* lasts throughout the Paschal season and is intended to provide the neophyte with the time and opportunity to develop a deeper understanding and appreciation of the mysteries of the faith after having participated in the sacraments for the first time.

Rituals of Initiation[23]

Ritually, the first liturgical celebration in the process of adult initiation is the Rite of Acceptance into the Order of Catechumens.[24] Solemnly marking the candidate's entrance into the catechumenate, this rite is celebrated in the presence of the assembled community. Before entering the church building, each candidate asks God's Church for that faith which leads to eternal life, and promises to follow the path of faith under the leadership of Jesus Christ:

> You have followed God's light and the way of the Gospel now lies open before you. Set your feet firmly on that path and acknowledge the living God, who truly speaks to everyone. Walk in the light of Christ and learn to trust in his wisdom. Commit your lives daily to his care, so that you may come to believe in him with all your heart.[25]

The community similarly promises to help the candidates know and follow Christ.[26]

Accompanied by their sponsors,[27] the candidates step forward and each one's forehead is signed with a cross:

> N., receive the cross on your forehead.
> It is Christ himself who now strengthens you
> with this sign of his love.
> Learn to know him and follow him.[28]

If it is deemed appropriate, the senses (ears, eyes, lips, breast, and shoulders) are also signed.[29] In countries where non-Christian religions flourish, the candidates may then be given a new name, and an episcopal conference may also elect to incorporate any other symbolic act which is a local custom and consonant with the purpose and meaning of the rite.

Then the catechumens and their sponsors are welcomed into the church for the celebration of the word of God:

> N. and N. come into the church,
> to share with us at the table of God's word.[30]

At the conclusion of the homily the celebrant may choose to present each catechumen with books containing the Gospels, after which the community joins in intercessory prayer for the catechumens:

> That they may undertake with generous hearts and souls whatever God may ask of them. . . .
> That they may have our sincere and unfailing support every step of the way. . . .
> That they may find in our community compelling signs of unity and generous love. . . .[31]

The ritual then calls for the dismissal of the catechumens. Upon first reading that, some people find it to be inappropriate to even consider dismissing catechumens. They regard such a dismissal as psychologically unsound—treating them as children to be banished, or regarding the community as an elite group. To a degree, both are true.

Catechumens are childlike to the extent that they are newcomers to the Word of God. In order for the Word to take root in their lives, it must not only be planted, but nurtured as well with time and care. One axis of dismissing the catechumens after the Liturgy of the Word, not only at the Rite of Acceptance into the Order of Catechumens, but at every communal celebration of the Eucharist, is to allow them the opportunity to reflect on the Liturgy of the Word together as a catechumenate community. The other axis clearly draws the line of distinction between the baptized and the non-baptized.

Our reluctance to dismiss catechumens for fear of offending them is understandable given our cultural conditioning. It was a catechumen, however, who helped me to understand the real importance of the dismissal.

Dave was the only catechumen in the small college community. This might easily be a situation in which pastoral reasons might preclude the dismissal of the catechumen, as the ritual permits.[32] Therefore, it surprised me when Dave said he actually wanted to leave after the homily: "I need time to think about what the Scriptures said. Father preached about what the Scriptures said to him, but sometimes I hear something different. If I don't think about these things at the time, they slip away from me. That time to be alone with the Word is the best part of my week!"

I was struck by Dave's comments and taken aback at the irony of my own reminiscences. I remember that the whole Liturgy of the Word was once dismissed from our attention in favor of the principal parts of the Mass. Dave's comments reminded me how far we have traveled since those days.

Dismissing catechumens, some think, makes an elitist community of the baptized. Surely baptism doesn't make us superior to the catechumens, but it certainly does make us different. To make the distinction heightens our awareness of the important place baptism has in our lives and in the life of the Church. Because so many of us were baptized as infants and often tend to take the sacrament of baptism for granted, we need such reminders of its power every now and then. Using the term sending forth to replace the disturbing concept of dismissing candidates and catechumens is gaining wider acceptance and seems to be more compatible with American sensitivities.[33]

The Catechumenate

Special celebrations of the Word, minor exorcisms, and anointings may be held during the course of the catechumenate. Here the RCIA gives a wide breadth of options, but the motivation behind celebrating these various rituals is to "purify the catechumens little by little and strengthen them with God's blessing."[34]

a. Celebrations of the Word are intended to help nurture the teachings the catechumens receive. These rituals also provide them with various experiences of community prayer, giving them a familiarity with our signs, celebrations, and seasons, and preparing them for membership in the worshipping community.[35]

b. The minor exorcisms are powerful examples of petitionary prayer directed to God by the community. The prayers refer to the struggles with which the Christian life is marked—"the struggle between flesh and spirit, the importance of self-denial for reaching the blessedness of God's kingdom, and the unending need for God's help."[36]

c. Although catechumens do not yet have the benefit of sacramental grace, blessings are intended to impart signs of God's love and the Church's care during the course of the catechumenate, giving courage, joy, and peace along the journey.[37]

d. Anointings may be celebrated periodically during the catechumenate. Traditionally oil is a powerful symbol for Christians, serving as God's mark of strength, and may be given on various parts of the body if it is deemed appropriate.[38]

e. The presentations, which will be discussed in the following section, may also be anticipated and celebrated during the catechumenate.[39]

Diocesan Celebrations of Election

The next major liturgical celebration is the Rite of Election or Enrollment of Names, which is commonly celebrated on the first Sunday of the Lent preceding baptism. This rite marks the end of the catechumenate, and the beginning of final preparation for the sacraments of initiation.

In many parts of the country, local ordinaries have begun to hold diocesan celebrations of the Rite of Election, since the bishop is the appropriate presider.[40] These should never be duplications of parish celebrations, but neither should the parish ignore the occasion when Election takes place at the cathedral. An optional ritual for the sending of the catechumens for election is provided in the RCIA.[41]

During this ritual the catechist or representative of the community calls forward the catechumens accompanied by their godparents. This is the first occasion on which the godparents publicly exercise their ministry. They are men and women chosen by the candidates for their witness to the Christian way of life. They are delegated by the community "to show the candidates how to practice the Gospel in personal and social life, to sustain the candidates in moments of hesitancy and anxiety, to bear witness, and to guide the candidates' progress in the baptismal life."[42] The celebrant then asks each of the godparents to testify regarding the candidate's "formation in the Gospel and in the Catholic way of life." They are also asked whether or not they regard the candidates ready to be presented to the bishop for the rite of election. After they give their consent the celebrant concludes the affirmation saying:

> My dear catechumens, this community gladly recommends you to the bishop, who, in the name of Christ, will call you to the Easter sacraments. May God bring to completion the good work he has begun in you. [43]

The community joins in the intercessory prayers for the catechumens, after which the elect are to be dismissed, while the community continues with the celebration of the Eucharist.

Rite of Election

This celebration begins with the Liturgy of the Word. After the homily, the catechumens are presented by the catechist, who asks the bishop that the catechumens be allowed to participate in the sacraments of baptism, confirmation, and Eucharist after celebrating the scrutinies. The catechumens, together with their godparents, are then called forward. Once again the godparents are asked to affirm the catechumen's readiness to be enrolled among the elect.

The catechumens are then asked to offer their names for enrollment. This part of the ritual may be carried out in a variety of ways. If there are a great number of candidates, the list may simply be presented to the bishop. If the number of candidates in the diocese is small they may be asked to inscribe their names in the Book of the Elect individually. If this had previously been done in parishes, of course, it is not duplicated at the cathedral.

The catechumens are then officially admitted to the ranks of the elect, and reminded of their duty to continue to strive toward their goal.

The godparents are likewise reminded of their responsibility to continue guiding the elect by their loving care and good example.

Following the intercessions for the elect, the celebrant, with hands outstretched over the elect, prays over them before the dismissal.

Purification and Enlightenment

The period of purification and enlightenment, which ideally coincides with Lent, is an important time in the life of the community. The many themes of Lent form a fitting backdrop to the preparation of the elect. Traditionally a time of repentance and renewal for all Christians, the spiritual recollection that frames the period of purification and enlightenment for the elect harmonizes easily with the penitential character of the larger community. The rituals that may be celebrated during this period, therefore, have great significance for the entire community.

The scrutinies take place on the third, fourth, and fifth Sundays of Lent, for which the lectionary readings of the A-cycle are specifically intended. These selections recount the stories of the Samaritan woman at the well, the curing of the man born blind, and the raising of Lazarus. After the homily on each of these Sundays, the elect and their godparents are called forward, and the elect are asked to demonstrate their spirit of repentance (by kneeling, bowing their heads, or by some other means). During the community prayer for the elect which follows, the godparents place their right hands on the shoulder of the one they are sponsoring. The community's intercessory prayer at each of these celebrations draws out elements that were present in the readings. The community prays, for example, that the elect may:

> like the woman of Samaria . . . review their lives before Christ and acknowledge their sins. . . .
>
> be freed from the spirit of mistrust that deters people from following Christ. . . .
>
> long with all their hearts for the living water that brings eternal life. . . .[44]

Each of the scrutinies concludes with a prayer of exorcism over the elect, the laying on of hands (if it can be done conveniently), and the dismissal of the elect:

> God of power,
> you sent your Son to be our Savior.
> Grant that these catechumens,
> who, like the woman of Samaria, thirst for living water,
> may turn to the Lord as they hear his word
> and acknowledge the sins and weaknesses that weigh them down.
> Protect them from vain reliance on self
> and defend them from the power of Satan.
> Free them from the spirit of deceit,
> so that, admitting the wrong they have done,
> they may attain purity of heart
> and advance on the way to salvation.[45]

If they were not anticipated during the catechumenate (second stage), the presentations take place in the presence of the community at weekday masses, for which special readings have been provided. The presentation of the Creed takes place during the week following the third scrutiny, and the presentation of the Lord's Prayer in the week following the fifth scrutiny. In both cases these presentations are made after the homily, and before a special community prayer for the elect. Once again the elect ought to be dismissed before the Liturgy of the Eucharist.

The RCIA also provides certain preparatory rites, some or all of which may be celebrated sometime on Holy Saturday, according to the celebrant's preference, the elect's needs, and the community's involvement. A series of readings is provided, but selections should be made according to those rites which will be used. These rites include recitation of the Creed, the rite of *ephpheta*, choosing a Christian name, and anointing with the oil of catechumens.

Sacramental Initiation

The apex of the initiation process, however, is the celebration of the sacraments of initiation, ideally at the Easter Vigil.[46] As the elect and their godparents approach the baptismal font, the celebrant asks the community to join in the litany of the saints, praying that the elect will be given the new life of the Holy Spirit. The blessing of the water is followed by the renunciation, anointing with the oil of catechumens,[47] and the profession of faith.

Baptism may be by immersion of the whole body, the head only, or by infusion. Thus the adult is either immersed three times by the celebrant or deacon, or the water is poured three times as the individual is baptized, "in the name of the Father, and of the Son, and of the Holy Spirit." Then the godparent places his or her right hand on the neophyte's shoulder while the community joins in singing a short acclamation. Each neophyte is then clothed with the white garment.

The neophytes also receive a candle lit from the paschal candle, which is presented to them by their godparents.

The sacrament of confirmation follows, but is separated from the sacrament of baptism by congregational singing and/or movement from the baptismal font to the sanctuary. The sacrament is conferred by the same person who conferred baptism.[48]

After this rite the neophytes, who have been dismissed in previous celebrations, participate fully in the general intercessions of the faithful and the liturgy of the Eucharist for the first time.

Mystagogy

There are no specific liturgical rites either during the mystagogical period, or to mark the end of it. It is suggested, however, that throughout the Paschal Season the neophytes, along with their godparents where that is possible, be seated in a special place among the faithful. Attention should continually be drawn to their presence and their commitment in the homily and in the general intercessions.[49]

The end of this post-baptismal catechesis should likewise be noted in some type of liturgical or extra-liturgical celebration, sometime around Pentecost.[50] Furthermore, if the bishop has not been present during the celebration of any of the rites, the RCIA urges him to meet with the newly baptized and to celebrate the Eucharist with them during the mystagogical period.[51]

Catechetical Content[52]

Catechetically, the pre-catechumenate is characterized by informal exchanges during which initial conversion crystallizes, and the inquirer is given some general information about the particular community. This might include introductions to the parish staff, who could present different aspects of parish life and the various types of organizations that operate within the parish. During this time each candidate will be given (or choose) a sponsor who will be a primary support person. He or she will come to know the candidate, so as to be able to testify publicly to the candidate's morals, faith, and intention at the Rite of Acceptance into the Order of Catechumens.

Formal catechesis is primarily the province of the second stage—the catechumenate. During this period the catechumens become acquainted with the doctrinal, practical, liturgical, and evangelical dimensions of the community and the Church itself. Guided by priests, deacons, catechists, and other individuals, the catechumens are led to understand the principal dogmas and precepts of the Church, and to appreciate the mystery of salvation. Formal discussion ought to be coupled with celebrations of the Word appropriate to the liturgical cycle. From other members of the community as well, especially sponsors and godparents, catechumens learn:

> to turn more readily to God in prayer, to bear witness to the faith, in all things to keep their hopes set on Christ, to follow supernatural inspiration in their deeds, and to practice love of neighbor, even at the cost of self-renunciation.[53]

The liturgical rites celebrated during the catechumenate help the catechumens to participate fruitfully in the Liturgy of the Word, and to anticipate eagerly their eventual celebration of the Liturgy of the Eucharist. Finally, by the example given them in this catechumenal process, they will have first-hand knowledge of how to spread the gospel to others.

In meetings held at regular intervals, the catechumens should be encouraged by the catechists who direct the course of the catechumenate to ask serious questions concerning faith and the commitment involved. Helping the catechumens during this period, however, is actually the responsibility of the entire community, for all members should witness to each of these ecclesial dimensions in their own lives. This responsibility can be adverted to in the general intercessions, as well as in homilies where appropriate. Because of the long span of time which the catechumenate covers, a firm bond between catechumens, catechists, and community leaders should be nurtured and developed, eventually leading the catechumens to play an active role in the community as full members.

The third stage in this catechetical process can best be characterized as a forty-day retreat. Although it would be unreasonable in most societies to expect that the elect would be able to leave their jobs and social responsibilities for such a prolonged period of time, it is not unrealistic to imagine individuals spending more time in prayer and less time in front of the television, or at least in the bowling alley.[54]

One local parish has designed a type of at home retreat for the elect to use during the period of enlightenment. The elect meet together with a director on Wednesday and Friday evenings, not for convenience, but to emphasize the Church's traditional days of penance. On Monday evenings, when possible, they also participate in the regular parish services, which consist of evening prayer and a brief homily.

The catechumenal team at St. Mary's has decided that it is better that the director of this process be someone who has been part of the process, but whose contribution has been associated with spiritual rather than catechetical formation. Their parish is fortunate enough to have a spiritual director on the team who guides this, as well as other parish retreats.

Once again, the intensity of this period of proximate preparation will be specifically determined by the needs of the elect, and intermediary liturgical rites which mark this stage help to focus the attention of the elect, their directors, and the community at large on the seriousness of their faith-commitment.

The Honeymoon

It has been a nagging fear of mine that our cultural tendency toward a quick wrap-up will dismiss the period of mystagogy. It is quite possible that the last stage—the mystagogical catechesis—might be eclipsed as a direct result of the intensity of the previous stage. After the jubilant celebration of the three sacraments of initiation, the natural tendency might be simply to end the process at the Easter Vigil. Spiritually and psychologically, however, a *denouement* is most essential, since the neophytes, whose lives have been radically changed, need time to reflect on those profound mysteries they have finally experienced. Not to plumb the depths of the experience at the time is to lose its impact forever.

Think of mystagogy as a post-baptismal honeymoon and you might understand its significance differently.

Dave, the young man whose experience taught me the importance of dismissing the catechumens, spent the week after his initiation at a Benedictine Monastery. There, hundreds of miles from his parish church, the sights, sounds, and odors of the Easter Vigil lingered in the air. He had an entire week to revel in its mystery and to enjoy his new relationship with God and the community of the baptized.

Conclusion

It is obvious from this survey that the Rite of Christian Initiation of Adults activates a process-relational model of the Church. As individuals become involved in the initiation process, they become part of the community's developmental process, which is central to the Church's developmental process.[55] This thrust is evident in *Gaudium et Spes:*

> [Our] social nature makes it evident that the progress of the human person and the advance of society itself hinge on each other. [From] the beginning, the subject and the goal of all social institutions is and must be the human person, which for its part and by its very nature stands completely in need of social life. This social life is not something added on to [a person]. Hence, through [our] dealings with others, through reciprocal duties, and through [communal] dialogue [we] develop all [our] gifts and are able to rise to [our] destiny.[56]

Not only does this afford us a renewed basis of understanding Church, but also a methodology for understanding how sacraments function in the lives of Christians.

NOTES

1. *See* note 2 in the Introduction of this book, p. 9.

2. The best documentation for this relates directly to the French Church, although the French situation was certainly not unique. The statistics revealed that baptism was being delayed, and in many cases not being administered to infants at all, necessitating the development of a more comprehensive ritual for use when baptism occurred at a later age. Cf. J. Potel, *Moins de baptemes en France. Porquoi?* (Paris: Les Editions du Cerf, 1974).

3. *Acta Apostolicae Sedis [AAS]* 54 (1962) 310-38.

4. *See* Frederick McManus, "The Restored Liturgical Catechumenate," *Worship* 36 (1962) 536-49; "Adult Baptism," *Worship* 37 (1963) 257-59; J. B. O'Connell, "The New Rite of Adult Baptism," *Clergy Review* 48 (1963) 352-62.

5. Constitution on the Sacred Liturgy [CSL] no. 64, in *The Documents of Vatican II,* ed. Walter M. Abbott (New York: America Press, 1966) 159.

6. CSL, no. 66, 159-60.

7. Decree on the Church's Missionary Activity [M] no. 14, 600–01; Decree on the Bishops' Pastoral Office in the Church [B] no. 14, 406; Decree on the Ministry and Life of Priests [P] no. 6, 543–46; Dogmatic Constitution on the Church [C] no. 14, 32–33.

8. *AAS* 56 (1964) 139–44. English translation by Frederick McManus, *Jurist* 24 (1964) 106.

9. To date no official account of the *Consilium*'s work has been issued. The sources used in this summary, therefore, are diverse: Jacques Cellier, "Le nouveau rite de l'initiation chretienne des adultes," *La Documentation Catholique* 69 (1972) 217–21; Andre Aubry, "Le projet pastoral du rituel de l'initiation des adultes," *Ephemerides Liturgicae* 88 (1974) 174–91; Jean-Baptiste Molin, "Le nouvel rituel de l'initiation chretienne des adultes," *Notitae* 8 (1972) 87–95; *Schemata* nos. 32, 77, 112, 147, 344, and 352 (private papers of *Coetus* 22).

10. The members of *Coetus* 22, who came from Germany [4], France [4], Belgium [2], Spain [1], and the United States [1], represented diverse areas of expertise, skilled in missionary and pastoral work, as well as liturgical history and theology, and their work progressed under the leadership of Balthasar Fischer and Jacques Cellier as *relatores*. An interesting account of the workings of other groups is found in Bernard Botte, *From Silence to Participation: An Insider's View of Liturgical Renewal*, trans. John Sullivan, O.C.D. (Washington: Pastoral Press, 1988).

11. Cellier, "Le nouveau rite de l'initiation chretienne des adultes" 217.

12. *Schemata* 32/*De Rituali* 1, no. 18.

13. *Ibid.* no. 19.

14. After World War II, statistics showed a considerable increase in France in the number of adults seeking baptism, which resulted from an increase in the number of non-baptized, and the fruition of various apostolic endeavors. Statistics further demonstrated, however, that eighty percent of those individuals did not persevere to baptism. Recognizing that the process of conversion presented serious difficulties for adults, Church leaders in France concluded that parish structures were unable to support the needs of such individuals. As an alternative, therefore, independent catechumenal communities were formed. *See* Francis Coudreau, "The Catechumenate in France," *Worship* 42 (1968) 223–42.

15. *Schemata* 77/*De Rituali* 2.

16. *Schemata* 112/*De Rituali* 5.

17. These included Japan, Mali, Togo, Ivory Coast, Upper Volta, Rwanda, Kinshasa, Belgium, Canada, France, and the United States.

18. While the questionnaires themselves were not available for study, their general thrust could be inferred from the report of the Vanves meeting which was forwarded for further comment to those catechumenal centers participating in the experiment.

19. The English translation [RCIA] by the International Commission on English in the Liturgy [ICEL], however, was not available until 1974.

20. Canon 851.1, *Code of Canon Law* (1983).

21. RCIA, no. 37.

22. RCIA, no. 47.

23. *See Commentaries on the Rite of Christian Initiation of Adults*, ed. James A. Wilde (Chicago: Liturgy Training Publications, 1988).

24. The RCIA does not specify a time for this celebration, but suggests that a day be chosen "according to local conditions," [no. 18]. The National Statutes for the Catechumenate, approved by the National Conference of Catholic Bishops in November of 1986, however, state that that period of the catechumenate (from acceptance into the order of catechumens to the rite of election) should "extend for at least one year of formation, instruction, and probation." They suggest, therefore, that the rite be celebrated before Lent in one year so that the time of formation can extend until Easter of the following year (no. 6).

25. RCIA, no. 52a.

26. In countries where "pagan worship" flourishes the conference of bishops may decide

to replace this rite of first acceptance of the Gospel with the rite of exorcism and the renunciation of false worship.

27. A sponsor is a member of the community who serves as a representative and a guide for the catechumen. The sponsor and the godparent may be one and the same person, but it is not necessary that they be so. This is a most important role in the process of Christian initiation and should not be delegated lightly. *See* Michel Dujarier, "Sponsorship," in *Adult Baptism and the Catechumenate*, Concilium, vol. 22, ed. Johannes Wagner (New York: Paulist Press, 1967); *Finding and Forming Sponsors and Godparents*, ed. James A. Wilde (Chicago: Liturgy Training Publications, 1988).

28. RCIA, no. 55a.

29. RCIA, no. 56.

30. RCIA, no. 60.

31. RCIA, no. 65.

32. *See* RCIA, no. 75.3.

33. *See* James B. Dunning, "Don't Dismiss the Dismissal: But Change the Name," *Church* 5/2 (Summer 1989) 34–37.

34. RCIA, no. 75.3.

35. RCIA, no. 82.

36. RCIA, no. 90.

37. RCIA, no. 95.

38. *See* RCIA, nos. 98–102.

39. RCIA, no. 103.

40. *See* RCIA, no. 108.

41. *See* RCIA, nos. 106–17.

42. RCIA, no. 11.

43. RCIA, no. 112.

44. RCIA, no. 140b. Cf. no. 154; no. 161.

45. RCIA, no. 141a.

46. In the case of serious pastoral need these celebrations may occur outside the Lent-Easter Cycle, but the arrangement of the rite remains the same.

47. If this rite has been anticipated in the preparatory rites, it is omitted here.

48. The priest-celebrant may also confirm those who are being received into full communion, but confirmation of those baptized as Catholics is still reserved to the bishop. *See* Canon 883, CIC. RCIA, no. 385.

49. RCIA, no. 238.

50. RCIA, no. 239.

51. RCIA, no. 241.

52. See *Before and After Baptism: The Work of Teachers and Catechists*, ed. James A. Wilde (Chicago: Liturgy Training Publications, 1988).

53. RCIA, no. 75.2.

54. *See* Richard W. Chilson, *A Lenten Pilgrimage—Dying and Rising in the Lord* (New York: Paulist Press, 1983).

55. Bernard Lee, *The Becoming of the Church* (New York: Paulist Press, 1974) 179.

56. *Gaudium et Spes* [GS] no. 25, 224.

CHAPTER FOUR

Shifting Sands of Sacramental Life

We began this study by examining not only the shape of the present world, but also the shape of the Church that emerged from the pages of the documents of Vatican II. From that vantage point, we looked back to the Church of the first millennium to see a world in turmoil and a Church being shaped and reshaped in response to the needs of that world. Finally, we turned our attention to the Rite of Christian Initiation of Adults, which has been heralded as the most radical document of the post-conciliar Church.[1] Although we examined the RCIA canonically, ritually, and catechetically, we have yet to attend to the radical impact this rite is having on our entire sacramental structure. It is the RCIA as model that will focus our celebration of sacraments in the next millennium.

In this chapter we will turn our attention to the effects the RCIA is already having on our entire sacramental structure. Although later chapters will develop in greater detail how sacramental preparation and celebration might build on the work of the RCIA in the next millennium, in this chapter our discussion will be limited to the effects themselves:

- a developing baptismal spirituality
- an appreciation for process in addition to product
- a deeper understanding and appreciation of the dynamics of sponsorship
- a developing sense of community among the faithful
- an enhanced understanding of Eucharist

In Search of a Spirituality

The closing decades of the twentieth century have witnessed the emergence of pop-psychology. In the seventies Gail Sheehy,[2] Wayne Dyer,[3]

and Leo Buscaglia[4] each authored several books that have not only domi-
nated the non-fiction best-seller lists, but have also helped millions of
people toward a better understanding of the dynamics of human behavior.
They have helped their readers to alter the course of their lives, improv-
ing the quality of their lives in the process. A year or so before he became
a national celebrity, Wayne Dyer gave a workshop for the faculty of the
high school where I was teaching. I vividly recall his shouting out to the
audience, "How many of you are nervous?" "How many of you worry?"
Still suffering from the delusion that anxiety was productive, faculty members enthusiastically raised their hands in response to each of his questions. After two hours with Dr. Dyer, however, we learned that we need
not be prisoners of our own anxiety. Actually we had many more choices
in life than we ever thought possible. We were ready to surrender our
roles as victims, and to take charge of our own lives.

Due to its tremendous success, pop-psychology has spawned a new
child—pop spirituality. It seems we have everything from a spirituality
of housework to a spirituality of the stock market. Ira Progoff has shown
us how to sacralize the past, the present, the future, our dreams, our imag-
ination, and every waking thought.[5] Cursillos, marriage encounters, weekend retreats, directed retreats, and thirty-day retreats all trigger a renewed
interest in things spiritual. More and more people are seeking spiritual
direction, and consequently more and more are studying its techniques.
New Age spirituality has now dawned, affecting medicine, music, food,
and religion in its glow. Everyone seems to be searching . . . but something essential is often missing in the search.

A few years ago we were all in the swing of the back-to-basics movement in education. What the RCIA virtually forces us to do is to apply
that principle to spirituality. Through the RCIA we are more firmly rooted
in our baptismal commitment, more conscious of the way of life to which
we committed ourselves in baptism.

Baptismal Spirituality

Obviously, the first difficulty we have in developing an appreciation of
our baptismal commitment is that for most of us there is simply no conscious recollection of making that commitment, or often even an understanding of it as *our* commitment. It was made in our name when we were
barely able to see. Many of us probably even slept peacefully through
the ceremony. That's precisely why the link is missing in the first place!
The ritual over and done with, the grace already flowing, rarely was it

considered important to return and understand either the dynamic or the full import of that commitment. Beyond learning to recite a definition of baptism, there seemed to be no other need to explore the sacrament, for we had already received it.

Once we have experienced the RCIA, however, either as sponsors or as members of the larger ecclesial community, the link between baptism and spirituality is no longer missing. Vicariously, through the journey of each new catechumen, every member of the community can enter once again into the mystery of salvation.[6] It no longer matters at what age the commitment was initially made, for we see the profound need for conversion personally, communally, and societally, played out before us through the rituals of the catechumenate. We do not have to search outside for a spirituality, for we recognize the response we gave to the call of Jesus by being incorporated into his community of faith. The character that was imprinted upon us at that time remains forever. The grace of baptism continues to strengthen us throughout our faith-life journey. Once we have learned again that baptism is the sacrament that gives shape and sense to the other sacraments, all sacraments will be celebrated with greater attention to that basic connection.

Christians in Process

Tertullian (c. 160–c. 230), whose writings have helped us to understand the growth of the Church of his day, is credited with having made the astute observation that "Christians are made, not born."[7] Although the context for his statement was a repudiation of the growing practice of infant initiation, his point is still well taken. Whether we were baptized as infants or initiated into the community as adults, each of us will continue to be in process as we journey though this earthly life. The moment of baptism marks the beginning of that journey.

In the days before Vatican II, we tended to see sacraments as end-points rather than as starting points. What seemed to concern us most was getting the grace flowing. To cite an extreme example, people in the Middle Ages had their children baptized within hours of birth not only to open the floodgates to grace, but also to preserve their children from the fate of limbo. The long-term cumulative effect of such an attitude toward baptism was that it became social rather than experiential. Baptism meant no more than membership in the Church.[8]

What we learn from the conciliar documents as well as our experience of the RCIA, however, is that process is a value in itself. Furthermore, by short-circuiting the process for the sake of expediency or convenience, we deny people the grace inherent in the process.

Our theology of grace is rich, and is not limited to moments of receiving the ritual sacraments. By understanding grace as a relationship that exists between God and the individual, we can more readily allow for the awareness of God's grace flowing throughout the process.

The effect of valuing process is already being seen in some of our sacramental programs, most notably confirmation and marriage. These will be examined in succeeding chapters, but in addition to those programs which are already in place, some theologians are suggesting that this understanding of process might also find application in the sacrament of penance.[9]

Sponsorship

The RCIA fosters the development of a multi-dimensional ministry of sponsorship: personal, spiritual, educational, and ecclesial. Although the degree of development given to each of these dimensions will depend on the persons involved, ideally the relationship will be mutually enriching given whatever degree of development is achieved.

The rite describes the role of sponsor as one who "accompanies any candidate seeking admission as a catechumen. Sponsors are persons who have known and assisted the candidates and stand as witnesses to the candidates' moral character, faith, and intention."[10]

On a personal level, therefore, the rite immediately designates the sponsor to be a companion. In analyzing the word from its Latin roots (com meaning "with" and panis meaning "bread") we see that the role of the sponsor is literally to eat bread with the catechumen. Socially, of course, this implies much more than simply sharing food. It includes sharing one's stories, hopes, feelings, dreams, and difficulties. In his recent book Megatrends, John Naisbitt, in outlining the needs of present-day society, states that a technologically advanced culture needs to have a corresponding degree of affectivity for balance. He names this thesis "high tech, high touch."[11] Given that analysis, sponsorship is the high touch component of the RCIA.[12]

Because sponsorship moves into the affective level, it can be spiritually enriching for both sponsors and catechumens. Sharing not only their personal experiences of God's movement in their lives, but also praying together and entering into the mystery of faith, can be profoundly moving. In my work with sponsors I hear countless stories of how deeply their relationship with God has been affected through the process of the RCIA. Harold, a sponsor, recently said to me, "I can't believe it! A decade of Marriage Encounter and yearly retreats seem to have brought me nowhere by comparison. Ed (his catechumen) actually engaged me in the mystery that is God. It's awesome!" Such testimonies abound where there is an active catechumenate.

Educationally, of course, the value of sponsorship is somewhat more obvious. Who of us wouldn't have benefited from a personal tutor as we went through school? In a sense, that is also part of the sponsor's role. Because of the relationship established between sponsor and catechumen, not only will the sponsor be equipped to answer the catechumen's questions, or to refer them to someone else who would have the answer, but the sponsor is also in a position to make connections between material learned and reality lived. Sponsors might also foresee potential problems or foster greater development.

Finally, there is an ecclesial component to the role of sponsor as well. Not only does the sponsor witness to the community in attesting to the catechumen's moral character, faith, and intention, as noted earlier, but the sponsor also serves as a witness to the catechumen. The sponsor gives witness to a personal life of faith in the community. In this way the sponsor becomes a representative not only *to* the Church but also *for* the Church. Not many will be called to shed blood as were the Church's first witnesses,[13] but the witness called forth in sponsorship implies laying aside one's own needs for the sake of the gospel. Surely, all of our sacraments could benefit from the component of sponsorship.

Building Community

An unmistakable by-product of the RCIA is the growth and strengthening of local Christian communities. This occurs in ever-widening circles, with the catechumens in the center, surrounded by their sponsors and others who form the base catechumenal community. From there the effect is extended throughout the parish community, much as one sees ripples extend after throwing a stone into a pool of water. The presence and prayer of the community support the catechumen, but along the way the community is strengthened by having developed a sense of corporate identity.

From its earliest days the Church has gathered people to itself and supported them with the presence of a community as they journeyed toward making a faith-commitment and becoming fully initiated members of the Christian community.

> The faithful all lived together and owned everything in common; they sold their goods and possessions and shared out of the proceeds among themselves according to what each one needed.
>   They went as a body to the temple every day but met in their houses for the breaking of bread; they shared their food gladly and generously; they praised God and were looked up to by everyone. Day by day the Lord added to their community those destined to be saved.[14]

This inevitably leads us back to the table around which we gather to celebrate our common commitment to the Gospel in the name of our Lord Jesus Christ.

Eucharist: Corporate Celebration of Faith

Christian liturgical tradition has always recognized the death and resurrection of the Lord Jesus to be its foundational principle, and the Eucharist to be the communal expression of that faith. It is equally important to note, however, that in the Roman Catholic tradition, practice has not always evidenced this fundamental belief. From the small group gathered around the table of the Lord, strengthened in the face of virulent persecution, we moved across the centuries to a privatized devotional experience of the Eucharist. In fact, today we still struggle to overcome the effects of the privatization of the Eucharist bequeathed to us by the counter-Reformation. The documents of Vatican II call us very clearly to return to the roots of our Christian heritage, to the Eucharistic tradition of celebrating our common faith:

> For it is through the liturgy, especially the divine Eucharistic Sacrifice, that "the work of our redemption is exercised." The liturgy is thus the outstanding means by which the faithful can express in their lives, and manifest to others, the mystery of Christ and the real nature of the Church.[15]

In his book, *The Eucharist and Human Liberation*, Tissa Balasuriya reminds us just how powerful this communal expression of faith could be. "The Eucharist has an extraordinary potential for being an agent of personal and global transformation. Every week about 200 million persons meet all over the world in Christian communities."[16] Two thousand years after Jesus' command, "do this in memory of me," we are only beginning to understand the staggering dimensions of what Jesus wants us to do.

Eucharist as Liturgy

When liturgy is seen as a pompous display of ecclesial wealth and power, it is not liturgy. When we talk about attending or hearing Mass, we are not describing liturgy. When we conclude that the obligation to attend the Eucharistic liturgy refers only to our physical presence, we have failed to understand what liturgy is all about. As Rafael Avila writes, "when Eucharist fails to exert any significance in the life of the Church, and when Christians feel estranged by the sacrament, something is seriously amiss."[17] Yes, something is seriously amiss—we do not know what liturgy is and what it can be for the People of God.

We know that in its Greek origins the word liturgy (*leitourgia*) literally meant "service for the sake of others." Serving in the army or caring for the destitute, in that sense, would have been considered liturgy. Since extant sources use the word in an exclusively religious context, however, liturgy has come to connote only religious service for the sake of others, or more properly, public worship. The well-hidden secret, you will agree, is often the concept that public worship is actually service rendered for others. From a ministerial perspective this would seem to be logical enough, but until the rituals of the RCIA, it has been difficult to express how each member of the congregation actually serves the whole assembly. In the past, liturgy was seen as something that was done for us—having Father say Mass for us. Consequently the worshipping community was placed in a position of relative passivity precisely when it was being called, in Eucharist, to be most authentically active.

This failure to understand the true nature of the liturgy is an age-old problem, and stems from two different roots. In one respect we have been plagued by the disease of minimalism for centuries, even in our *ex opere operato* sacramental theology. Nine first Fridays, five first Saturdays, slipping into Mass for the three principal parts, getting the Office in by mumbling Lauds at 11 p.m., we were mired in a spirituality of getting by. Were we so different from our relic-hungry, indulgence-hoarding ancestors? Salvation was a privatized affair. We had traveled far from the dinner table that night in the upper room.

Another root of our problems of misunderstanding the liturgy lies in the very architecture of our churches—an architecture that spoke a body language of passivity. From intimate gatherings of the faithful in house churches in the first three centuries, by the twelfth century the altar—the common table—had moved to a back wall and another wall had grown up, physically separating the community from the celebration. Until recently we have suffered from that distant alienation, and still neither ritual reform nor architectural renovations have managed to overcome its effects completely.

Eucharist in Early Christianity

A persecuted people, the first Christians gathered in their homes to celebrate the Eucharist—to remember Jesus, his message, and his mission. It was the Eucharist and the community gathered in celebration that strengthened and sustained them in those terrible days of persecution. This was their collective remembering of what it meant to have one's body broken and blood shed for another. Eucharist was the center of their lives.[18]

Always their plea, *"Maranatha!"* They were a people of faith. They believed deeply in the Lord Jesus, trusted that he would return, and worked at the risk of their very lives to live the way Jesus lived until his return. There was, therefore, an important social dimension to their celebration of the Eucharist. They brought offerings for "orphans and widows, and those who were in bonds, and strangers who were sojourners among them, and . . . all those in need."[19] From the celebration, furthermore, they went to bring the sacred bread to the sick and the infirm, showing us that this sharing was an integral rather than a secondary element of their Eucharistic feast.

Outlawed, persecuted, hunted down, these Christian ancestors of ours were making a political statement in their Eucharists. Ronald Marstin writes:

> Wherever faith is bent on building the truly reconciled as distinct from merely pacified society, the Eucharists will be divisive, exposing the discrepancies between the gospel we profess and the oppression we tolerate, and pressing us to align ourselves either with those who would change the system or those who would resist the change.[20]

So spoke the Lord Jesus: "Do you suppose that I am here to bring peace on earth? No, I tell you, but rather division" (Luke 12:51). So, the first Christians lived and died.

Thematic Development

Having uncovered the original intention of liturgy, looked at the development of the Eucharist, and reflected on New Testament Eucharistic spirituality, we see some specific themes emerge in the context of seeing Eucharist as a corporate work done in faith: hunger, presence, memory, renewal, and vocation.

Eucharist and Hunger

There is something fundamentally human about sharing a meal. Rarely do we come together and not eat. Our guests are barely in the door before we ask, "May I get you something to drink? Would you like something to eat?" Although we don't often reflect on the significance of those familiar words, this ritual has two dimensions. First, we are responding to hunger, and second, we are sharing ourselves and our resources. Distinctions are erased, barriers are lowered, injuries are healed, and enemies are reconciled as people gather together to break bread.

While the Last Supper was surely the most significant meal Jesus shared with his friends, it certainly was not the only meal recorded in Scripture. Understanding these meals helps us to see more clearly how Jesus used the occasion of a meal. We find a whole meal ministry, in fact, that enables us to deepen our understanding of Eucharist.[21] We know, for example, that Jesus taught and forgave at meals, often breaking bread with people whose reputations were less than respectable in the society of that day. The table sharing of Jesus, therefore, is yet another reflection of his preaching of the reign of God, where barriers between God and sinners would be destroyed. "The reality symbolized by the Eucharist," writes Michael Crosby, "is to be normative for the Church's life. All people are equal because all share in the one meal as tablemates."[22]

Throughout the months (or years) of the catechumenate, the community has stood by as the catechumens, and later the elect, have been dismissed (or sent forth) from the Sunday celebration. Clearly they have seen the distinction made between those who are baptized and those who are not, subtly reinforcing the significance of membership in the community.

In coming to the Eucharistic meal we testify to our common belief that it is the Lord Jesus who sustains and nourishes us, and pledge that we will likewise sustain and nourish one another with the bread that is our lives. That is our pledge to humanity. In his address to the 41st International Eucharistic Congress in Philadelphia in 1976, Fr. Pedro Arrupe reminded us that "if there is hunger anywhere in the world, then our celebration of the Eucharist is somehow incomplete everywhere in the world."[23] The move toward completing our celebration of the Eucharist in the long run, therefore, will necessitate addressing the issue of world hunger as a community of faith in a concrete way.

Eucharist and Presence

Eucharist is also an immersion in the mystery of presence. For nearly two thousand years now Jesus has been present to those who believe as they gather in his memory. True, there have been myriad explanations for this phenomenon—theologies galore—but, while scholars grapple with finding the intellectual construct capable of expressing the inexpressible, the people of faith have been grasped by the mystery—lured into the passion of presence. "I will be with you all days, even to the end of the world," Jesus promised. We trust the promise because we have known love, and it is love that leads us to plumb the mystery of presence.

Our theologizing about the mystery of real presence in the Eucharist has often been sadly incomplete. Once again, caught in the trap of minimalism, we have been duped into thinking that real presence is simply a definition or a doctrine and not primarily an experience that draws us as individuals and as community into the Godhead.

Beginning and ending with the doctrine, however, is only part of this limitation, because the mystery of presence in the Eucharist actually goes beyond the presence of Jesus—another dimension of the mystery upon which we rarely reflect. The ritual itself leads us beyond the presence and enhances the quality of presence because ritual time is a journey into the *kairos*. That unity of timelessness allows one experience to build on another, and to deepen the phenomenon of presence. There in that time-beyond-time, we join our tablemates—the community of the baptized of yesterday, today, and tomorrow, gathered from all the corners of the earth. The words of the third Eucharistic prayer remind us:

> From age to age you gather a people to yourself,
> so that from east to west
> a perfect offering may be made
> to the glory of your name.

Keeping Memory

It is inescapable that Eucharist also memorializes the passion and death of the Lord Jesus, for it is in the Eucharist that the sacrifice of the cross receives its meaning. "Viewed theologically, the passion of Jesus was the consequence of his fidelity to his Father and his fellow human beings," writes Leonardo Boff.[24] As a memorial, then, Eucharist is also an uncomfortable reminder to us of where the consequences of our fidelity might lead. When Jesus finished the Last Supper, he said, "Let us go to the Garden of Olives," and we know where that path led. The community gathered with us has watched the catechumens follow Jesus, which leads us to ask ourselves where we are willing to go.[25]

Eucharist as Renewal

The words Jesus used at the Last Supper renewed the covenant—God's promise to be with us through time, now in the presence and memory of God incarnate. It called to mind another meal—a meal of promise—celebrating another time when Yahweh-God intervened in history to redeem and liberate an oppressed people. The liberation which God wrought for God's people was a political revolution—a violent political revolution. It prefigured the subsequent liberation of the whole of humanity in Christ. Yahweh-God has been faithful to the covenant, which reached its ultimate expression in the death and resurrection of the Lord Jesus. It did not, however, end there, for it continues being renewed again and again as Christians gather together in the Lord's name.

Giving oneself (*doulouein*) involves liturgical overtones, for it is both a style of life and a liturgical expression that is connected to total submission to another.[26] Breaking the Eucharistic bread and distributing it is not only recognizing that Christ's gift is meant for everyone, it is also joining personally in the play of giving. "To participate in the Eucharist," writes Andre Foisson, "is to be invited to make the same journey; not only to exchange goods and words, but also to bring our very life into the system of giving."[27]

It was that dimension of the life of the Church that the bishops of Vatican II were attempting to address in their renewal of the liturgy:

> No Christian community . . . can be built up unless it has its basis and center in the celebration of the most Holy Eucharist. Here, therefore, all education in the spirit of community must originate. If this celebration is to be sincere and thorough, it must lead to various works of charity and mutual help, as well as to missionary activity and to different forms of Christian witness.[28]

The call for radical changes in the liturgy, therefore, did not stem from a diminished devotion to Jesus, but rather from a deeper understanding of the nature of the priesthood of Jesus which by baptism we promise to continue.[29]

Renewing our covenant as expressed in the Eucharist today, therefore, requires also a new approach to ecclesial life: deep personal and interpersonal reflection, new theological accents, socio-political analysis and options, action and evaluation, forming of alliances, risk-bearing, new lifestyles, new modes of being a Christian community, and a spirituality of the person and of the human community.[30]

In his book *The Spirituality of the Beatitudes*, Michael Crosby illustrates the cycles into which this places the Christian community. First, one has an experience that jars the worldview which has previously guided one's life. This leads one to call into question the very ideology that at another time undergirded one's understanding of existence—the world and God. Rejecting this former concept of God, one returns to the source—to Scripture—in search of similar experiences others might have had. Here one finds a new understanding of God, who is now revealed as part of this new experience of the world, part of one's life, and part of the life of the world.[31] This is the cycle we have seen operative in the life of the Church through the documents of Vatican II, and in the lives of many new Christians through the stages of the RCIA.

Eucharist: Our Vocation

Eucharist is also ultimately a call—a call for Christians to serve and to celebrate. This is not a reality which can be effected overnight, it has been found. Ritual renewal has been part of the process, as has architectural design, but at root has been the challenge to conversion. Looking back to the New Testament, we saw that for Jesus the Eucharist was fundamentally action-oriented. Balasuriya describes it as a "fundamental option to die rather than to live with compromise," for Jesus trusted in the survival of his message, not his body.[32] Celebrating the Eucharist and bringing about the reign of God, it follows, demands that we experience that same confidence in God's presence that we may be continually converted to God's authority.

Through the process of the RCIA the American Church has had an extraordinary experience of *koinonia*. We have come to know that spirit of community that compels us to serve and to celebrate in and through the Eucharist. We have seen that in the early Church the community was not a gathering of the "already converted," but the place where people lay themselves open to genuine conversion.[33] Father Arrupe sees that this unfolding reality of Eucharistic commitment is calling us to a new form of solidarity.

Eucharistic Solidarity

In the Eucharist we receive Christ hungering in the world. He comes to us, not alone, but with the poor, the oppressed, the starving of the earth. Through him, they are looking to us for help, for justice, for love expressed in action. Therefore, we cannot properly receive the Bread of Life unless at the same time we give bread for life to those in need wherever and whoever they may be.[34]

Over the centuries what has happened has been a gradual decline of common meaning.[35] The death and resurrection of the Lord Jesus is the paradigmatic event for the Christian community. The early Church endeavored to preserve and to prolong that event within the community by means of signs, symbols, sacred texts, music, and dance, forming a ritual. Prolonging, savoring the event that gave them identity as a people was the natural expression of the Christian community. They were compelled to celebrate—obligated by identity rather than by law. That is the point to which the Christian community will return, given the impact of the RCIA. The process is enabling us to see once again that Eucharist is *the* event of the Christian people, as the remembering necessary to continue the ministry of Jesus, as the celebration of active, continuous concern for others. The interior change this manifests will be so overwhelming that it will make the external changes in our liturgical celebration seem insignificant by comparison.

Conclusion

We have examined the RCIA in great detail, in both its historical and ecclesial contexts. This close examination has shown that the process-relational model of initiation seems responsive to the needs of our time and culture. What, however, does that do to the rest of our sacramental economy? Does the advent of the RCIA sound the death knell for infant baptism? Will confirmation celebrated apart from baptism cease to exist? It is to these questions that we will now turn our attention.

NOTES

1. *See* Aidan Kavanagh, "The Norm of Baptism: The New Rite of Christian Initiation of Adults," *Worship* 48 (1974) 143–52.

2. Gail Sheehy, *Passages: Predictable Crises of Adult Life* (New York: Dutton, 1976); *Pathfinders* (New York: Morrow, 1981).

3. Wayne Dyer, *Pulling Your Own Strings* (New York: Crowell, 1978); *Your Erroneous Zones* (New York: Funk & Wagnalls, 1976); *The Sky's the Limit* (New York: Simon & Schuster, 1980).

4. Leo Buscaglia, *Living, Loving, and Learning* (New York: Holt, Rinehart and Winston, 1982); *Love* (Thoroughfare, N.J.: Slack, 1982); *Loving Each Other: The Challenge of Human Relationships* (New York: Holt Rinehart and Winston, 1984); *Personhood: The Art of Being Fully Human* (Thoroughfare, N.J.: Slack, 1978).

5. *See* Ira Progoff, *At a Journal Workshop: The Basic Text and Guide for Using the Intensive Journal* (New York: Dialogue House, 1975); *The Practice of Process Meditation* (New York: Dialogue House, 1981).

6. *See Conversion and the Catechumenate,* ed. Robert Duggan (New York: Paulist Press, 1984).

7. *De Testimonio Animae* I.

8. Joseph Martos, *Doors to the Sacred: A Historical Introduction to Sacraments in the Catholic Church* (Garden City: Doubleday, 1981) 183.

9. The North American Forum on the Catechumenate in Washington, through its "Remembering Church" process, is presently exploring links between the process-relational model of the RCIA and penitential practice.

10. RCIA, no. 10. The sponsor is not necessarily the same person who will function as godparent in the later rites of the catechumenate and in the actual celebration of baptism.

11. John Naisbitt, *Megatrends: Ten New Directions Transforming Our Lives* (New York: Warner, 1982) 35–52.

12. Julia Upton, *Journey into Mystery: A Companion to the RCIA* (New York: Paulist Press, 1986) 32–34.

13. In Greek, the original of the New Testament, "witness" translates as *martyr.*

14. Acts 2:44-47.

15. Constitution on the Sacred Liturgy [CSL] no. 2.

16. Tissa Balasuriya, *The Eucharist and Human Liberation* (Maryknoll: Orbis, 1979) 132.

17. Rafael Avila, *Worship and Politics* (Maryknoll: Orbis, 1981) 2.

18. *Ibid.* xii.

19. Justin, First Apology, no. 67, *Early Christian Fathers,* ed. Cyril C. Richardson (New York: Macmillan, 1970) 175.

20. Ronald Marstin, *Beyond Our Tribal Gods: The Maturing Faith* (Maryknoll: Orbis, 1979) 45.

21. Paul Bernier, *Bread Broken and Shared: Broadening Our Vision of the Eucharist* (Notre Dame: Ave Maria Press, 1981) 27.

22. Michael Crosby, *Spirituality of the Beatitudes: Matthew's Challenge for First-World Christians* (Maryknoll: Orbis, 1981) 154.

23. Pedro Arrupe, "The Hunger for Bread . . .," *Address to the 41st International Eucharistic Congress,* Philadelphia, 1976.

24. Leonardo Boff, *Way of the Cross—Way of Justice* (Maryknoll: Orbis, 1980) ix.

25. *See* John H. Westerhoff, "Contemporary Spirituality: Revelation, Myth and Ritual," *Aesthetic Dimensions in Religious Education,* ed. Gloria Durka and Joanmarie Smith (New York: Paulist Press, 1979) 24–25.

26. Crosby, *Spirituality of the Beatitudes* 61.

27. Andre Foisson, "The Eucharist as an Act of Exchange," *Lumen* 35 (1980) 416.

28. Decree on the Ministry and Life of Priests, no. 6.

29. Balasuriya, *The Eucharist and Human Liberation* 118.

30. *Ibid.* 133.

31. Crosby, *Spirituality of the Beatitudes* 15.

32. Balasuriya, *The Eucharist and Human Liberation* 17.

33. Jim Wallis, *A Call to Conversion* (San Francisco: Harper and Row, 1981) 109.

34. Arrupe, "The Hunger for Bread . . ."

35. *See* Edward K. Braxton, *The Wisdom Community* (New York: Paulist Press, 1980).

Upton, Julia. *A Church for the Next Generation. Sacraments in Transition.* Collegevillem MN: The Liturgical Press, 1990.

CHAPTER FIVE

A Future for Infant Baptism

Infant Baptism has been so deeply rooted in our lives that it is astonishing for us to consider that in both the Roman Catholic and the Reformed traditions the baptism of infants has long been regarded as a practice in search of a theology. While some theologians have contended that the practice and theology both find their origin in the New Testament, others will contend that since a confession of faith is required for baptism, infants are automatically excluded from consideration.

Joachim Jeremias[1] and Oscar Cullman,[2] two of the major figures in this debate, each attempted to find New Testament evidence to support their position. Jeremias contended that evidence for the baptism of children dated no farther back than Tertullian in the second century, but that neither Tertullian nor any of his contemporaries gave a specific indication that infant baptism was an innovation in their day. Both Cullman and Jeremias cited ambiguous New Testament references,[3] but while Cullman saw these as absolute proof of the practice of baptizing infants in the era of the New Testament, Jeremias saw only the possibility of that being true.

Kurt Aland[4] approached the question from the perspective of early Church history, but although he absolutely denied that there was any evidence of infant baptism in the New Testament, he did not contend that this should preclude the possibility and validity of infant baptism today. Karl Barth,[5] on the other hand, centered his examination of the problem around the essential element of faith, forcefully asserting that since infants have no cognate ability, which an act of faith requires, they should not be baptized.

Although the debate continues at the present time, there are certain areas where we can find agreement in debate. Indiscriminate baptism of infants, for example, is generally rejected by all who are concerned with this issue. Several contemporary theologians have proposed that enrolling infants into a catechumenate, rather than baptizing them, might be responsive to both sides of the issue, and more closely aligned with a contemporary understanding of baptism.[6]

Now that the Rite of Christian Initiation of Adults has become mandatory, the development of the children's catechumenate will complicate the issue even further. It will raise serious questions regarding conflicting theologies that differing sacramental practices seem to imply. Let us begin our study of this subject by examining the pastoral reality of infant baptism today. This will put us in a better position to approach understanding the children's catechumenate as a liturgical structure for the next generation.

Infant Baptism and the Sacramental Economy

The Constitution on the Sacred Liturgy was promulgated on December 4, 1963, making it the first constitution issued by Vatican II. This document mandated a reform of the initiation rites:

> The rite for the baptism of infants is to be revised, and should be adapted to the circumstance that those to be baptized are, in fact, infants. The role of parents and godparents, and also their duties, should be brought out more sharply in the rite itself.[7]

The revised rite was published on May 5, 1969, and became effective in the dioceses of the United States on September 8, 1969. In the Introduction, careful attention is given to the area of parental preparation, and concern is shown for the continuing religious formation of those infants baptized:

> Before the celebration of the sacrament, it is of great importance that parents, moved by their own faith or with the help of friends or other members of the community, should prepare to take part in the rite with understanding.[8]

In order to achieve this goal, the rite recommends that parents be given appropriate books and instructions. Specific instructions to the parish priest are also given:

> The parish priest should make it his duty to visit them, or see that they are visited, as a family or as a group of families, and prepare them for the coming celebration by pastoral counsel and common prayer.[9]

Both documents, therefore, reinforce the necessity of faith on the part of those who bring the child to the sacrament, and on the part of those who accept the child into the community. Questions arise, however, when we see no evidence of faith. Several years ago, you might recall, a New England pastor refused to baptize the infant child of a Planned Parenthood advocate. Although that is the way it was reported in the media, the Church does not refuse baptism to any child. The Rite of Baptism for Children, however, clearly does make allowance for deferring baptism where the parents' faith is absent or questionable:

> When parents are not yet ready to profess the faith or to undertake their duty of bringing up their children as Christians, it is for the parish priest, keeping in mind whatever regulations may have been laid down by the conference of bishops, to determine the time for the baptism of infants.[10]

In fact, the crux of the so-called infant baptism debate is probably not infants at all, but adults. As Mark Searle has written, "If there is any reason for not admitting an infant to faith and baptismal life in the communion of the Church, it may only be that the child's own God-given household is not faithful."[11]

Lumen Gentium characterizes the Church as a robust community of believers inextricably bound together by their faith-commitment to Jesus Christ in one another:

> God has gathered together as one all those who in faith look upon Jesus as the author of salvation and the sources of unity and peace, and has established them as the Church, that for each and all she may be the visible sacrament of this saving unity.[12]

This has made Catholics more aware that they should at least be beginning to think of themselves as a community, even if they are not yet in reality a community. Experience has taught us time and again that before our actions will change, we must first change our attitudes.

At a recent diocesan congress I gave a lecture on the sacrament of penance. One man in the audience complained that on more than one occasion he had waited in church for the entire time assigned for confessions, and no priest ever arrived.

"Did you go over to the rectory?" I asked.

"No, I never thought of it," the man replied.

Until that man begins to think that he is as much a part of the Church as Father is, he will never ring the rectory doorbell to say, "There must be some mistake. None of the priests is hearing confessions."

The renewed emphasis on Scripture studies in the last few decades has begun to restore for us a strong biblical concept of faith—an adult faith flowing from personal conversion and repentance. The theology that follows from these convictions sees the sacraments as expressions of faith, and by correlation, faith as a necessity for the sacraments. This theological framework has been described by Karl Rahner:

> In the situation of a complex society made up of heterogeneous elements and of a diaspora extending through the whole of that society, the Church necessarily changes from a Church of regional and national communities to a Church of believers. What we mean by this is that the members of a Christian community constitute this community not solely in virtue of the continuity of office and the stability of the institutions governing the relationships between those members. . . . A further factor is precisely this free personal decision of faith which each member has won his or her way to in striving to come to terms with the pluralistic environment. Without impugning the sacramental significance of baptism (including infant baptism) it can be said that for the purpose of the concrete social realities of this environment the Christian community no longer depends (or at least depends less and less) upon such baptism and the ecclesiastical institutions as such, but rather on the free exercise of faith.[13]

Although in this context infant baptism makes more sense where there is strong parental and communal faith to support the child in the growth of faith, it makes us seriously question the sense of conferring a sacrament of faith if all that is being ritualized is a social convention, a celebration of birth, or a magical rite of instant salvation.

"Instant" Baptism

The faith that is described in relation to infant baptism is regarded as being three-dimensional:

Child

a. In one respect there is the incipient faith of the child. While the gift and the grace of faith might be present in the infant, as with other gifts and talents, it is only discernible with human growth and development.

Parent

b. Another dimension of faith is the matured faith of the parent. Of course, not all faith matures, so one might find many adults with the incipient faith still undeveloped. Consequently, it is unrealistic to expect that all parents will have mature faith.

Community

c. The most dynamic aspect of faith, however, is the corporate faith of the community. This is the most powerful dimension because it is the age-old faith, witnessed by the community of the apostles—the distinguishing characteristic of the universal Church.

Even if one dimension is lacking, the presence of the others is thought to be sufficient, so concern is usually centered on whether or not the minimum faith-quotient is present. Minimalism suffices when we might otherwise be engaged in seeking to develop and expand each of the three dimensions to its fullest.

During the last trimester of her pregnancy, my friend Ellen began to think seriously about her baby's baptism. Although when questioned about her religion Ellen would always admit to having been "raised Catholic," she was not married in the Church and had not "practiced" her religion in over ten years. In fact the only reason she was even considering having the child baptized was to placate her mother.

Shortly after her son was born, I was surprised when Ellen discussed her concerns with me. Since I knew she hadn't shadowed the door of the church since her graduation from the parish grammar school, and had some very strong feelings about the Catholic Church's position on many issues, I didn't think she would ever consider raising a child in the Church community. I asked her to describe what she really wanted for her son, Christopher.

"I want him to know and love God, to love and reverence the created world. I would like to have a ritual in our front room where the sun pours in. I would have water and plants and flowers around, because they are part of God's creation. Only the close family would be invited and we would join in dedicating Christopher to God. I know that would never satisfy Mother, though, so I'm thinking about having Christopher baptized."

She talked more about her experience of God and described who she understood Jesus to be. Her answers showed her to be a person of faith, although we would probably not characterize it as mature Christian faith. For that reason I suggested she discuss her dilemma with one of the parish priests we both knew. She and her husband met with the priest several times over the course of the next few months, struggling with questions of doctrine and the challenge of the Gospel.

When Ellen reached what Father Ed considered to be the minimum faith-quotient, he suggested they baptize Christopher. Still more concerned with appeasing her mother than celebrating a sacrament of faith, Ellen agreed to the baptism.

I attended the baptism, but images of the ritual Ellen originally described flashed in the back of my mind throughout the Mass. If Father Ed hadn't been satisfied with a minimum faith-quotient, perhaps Ellen would have come to see that in baptism Christopher was being embraced by God and the community. As it was, Ellen has not yet been able to see beyond her own capitulation to her mother's iron will, and the saddest part to me was that it marked the end of her search, at least for the moment.

Pastoral Reality

In actuality infant baptism places a heavy educative and formative obligation on both the family and the faith community. The Faith and Order Commission of the World Council of Churches, of which the Roman Catholic Church is a member, issued a statement emphasizing the context for infant baptism in the participating churches:

wcc

> stress is laid upon the corporate faith, upon an environment of faith, rather than upon the explicit decision of the recipient of baptism. Here the whole community affirms its faith in God and pledges itself to provide such an environment of faith, in the home, and in the worship, instruction and witness of the Church.[14]

In reality, however, this intrinsic element of responsibility is apt to be neglected, precisely because it seems to be virtually impossible to devise an adequate barometer of faith. Instead, we tend to rely on the culture, the parish school, and other religious organizations to serve as the locus for Christian formation.[15]

Baptism as Social Convention

Discussions with parents, those who are not "visible" members of the community and do not participate in its sacramental life, concerning their reasons for having their children baptized give us some very interesting information. Some weary parents trust that old fallacy that once they are baptized, children sleep through the night. Christiane Brusselmans has concluded that an analysis of the mentality of both practicing and non-practicing parents reveals that a great majority see in baptism a response to the vital needs of all people: the need to belong to a clearly-defined sociological group, and the need to provide for the security of their offspring.[16] Rather than being condemned as insufficient or theologically incorrect, these concepts could lead to the formation of a strong foundation upon which a better understanding of the Church might be built.

We cannot deny the fact that the Roman Catholic community is a sociological group, and as such helps to frame a person's identity. The most astute theologizing cannot change that human reality. Furthermore, as our society grows to be more technically complex, so does our need for the security that a sociological group can provide. Jesus knew that we would never be able to follow his path alone, and so he modeled for us a company of believers who encouraged and comforted, challenged and chastized each other. In a world that denied them the freedom to practice their religion openly, the community was their means of personal liberation.

> In other words, friends, through the blood of Jesus we have the right to enter the sanctuary, by a new way which he has opened for us, a living opening through the curtain, that is to say, his body. And we have the supreme high priests over all the house of God. So as we go in, let us be sincere in heart and filled with faith, our minds sprinkled and free from any trace of bad conscience and our bodies washed with pure water. Let us keep firm in the hope we profess, because the one who made the promise is faithful. Let us be concerned for each other, to stir a response in love and good works. Do not stay away from the meetings of the community, as some do, but encourage each other to go; the more so as you see the Day drawing near. (Heb 10:19-25)

Original Sin and Limbo

Although pre-baptismal instructions attempt to eliminate theological misconceptions occasioned by an inadequate understanding of original sin and limbo, they are often unable to achieve their purpose, either because they are too brief or too few in number, or because of the nature and accumulated psychological impact of these misconceptions. Some people truly believe that without baptism their child will suffer some pain of loss. Parents whose focus and terminology remain fixated in such a rigid understanding of the effects of original sin see that life without the beatific vision can only be one of punishment. Therefore, with an eye to giving their children the best possible life and protecting them from unforeseen dangers, regardless of their personal faith-commitment, these parents continue to request baptism for its cleansing rather than its incorporating aspect. Their concentration is focused on what could happen if their children were not baptized, rather than on the responsibility and faith-commitment assumed if their children are baptized.

There is growing evidence that Catholics have begun to rise above the "poor banished children of Eve" mentality, and consequently their understanding of original sin, along with other Catholic concepts, has also begun to evolve.[17]

An older woman in my class one day said, "I believed in limbo until my first child died at birth. Without any doubt, I knew my son was with God."

✓ Fear of limbo, which never rose above the category of a theological speculation, has been overshadowed in the post-Vatican II era by trust in God's loving providence. This is not to negate the understanding of original sin that has developed over time. What we experience instead is a change in emphasis.

When a child dies before receiving the sacrament of baptism, we commend the child to God's mercy, praying:

> God of all consolation,
> searcher of mind and heart,
> the faith of these parents [N. and N.] is known to you.

> Comfort them with the knowledge
> that the child for whom they grieve
> is entrusted now to your loving care.
> We ask this . . .[18]

Today stress is laid more on the interpersonal nature of original sin, naming original sin as the point of origin for this sinful, egocentric society in which we live. Through the water of baptism, the child is incorporated into a theo-centric community, which is attempting to overcome that sinful orientation of humanity which constitutes original sin.[19] Had not God intervened, being born into the human race would have destined one for an existence of egotism, alienation, and isolation. The effects of original sin remain even for the baptized Christian, for temptation to sin and sin itself continue. Ideally, the Christian community, composed of individuals who are theo-centric rather than egocentric, helps each member to counteract the effects of original sin in his or her own life. Regardless of the quality of community life, or the strength of individual faith, reversal of the sinful orientation that results from original sin has only been partly achieved, and is dependent on the grace of God, made visible in Jesus and in his Church, for complete realization.

Role of the Faith Community

Lisa's story convinced me of the importance of the faith community. She had been baptized as an infant, but her parents never participated in worship services. When Lisa reached school age, her parents enrolled her in the parish school, believing that she would be safer there than in the public school.

When her first grade teacher reminded the children to attend Mass on Sunday, Lisa wasn't sure what the teacher meant. Her friends, though, helped to clear up the mystery for her. Lisa began badgering her parents to take her to church. Since both were devoutly alienated from the Church by that time, they refused to attend themselves. But to appease their strong-willed daughter, they let her attend with her friends' families, or occasionally drove her to Mass themselves and picked her up an hour later, until she was old enough to travel the few blocks alone.

By the time I met Lisa she was a sophomore in college, and an active member of her parish community. She taught religion to young children on Saturday mornings and sang with the parish folk group. Never in her nineteen years had her parents ever come to church with her—not to her First Communion, First Penance, or Confirmation. The faith community supported her, strengthened her, and provided her with a religious identity.

Aside from her remarkable story, what also impressed me about Lisa was her loving regard for her parents. She never disparaged their inability to support her faith, but rather extolled their willingness to let her discover a home among God's people.

Infant baptism, administered to children of active members of the Christian community, can have profound meaning for parents and the ecclesial community alike, and therefore continues to occupy an important place in the sacramental life of the Church. As a practice it gives dramatic testimony to the power of faith, for parents, godparents, and the entire community are solemnly entrusted with the responsibility of forming the child in faith:

> You have asked to have your children baptized. In doing so you are accepting the responsibility of training them in the practice of the faith. It will be your duty to bring them up to keep God's commandments as Christ taught us, by loving God and our neighbor.[20]

Regardless of Lisa's story, baptizing the child of anyone who requests the sacrament, facilely accepting even a questionable degree of faith as sufficient, can rob the sacrament of its ritual dynamism. While this situation cannot negate the expression of faith witnessed in the baptism of a child whose parents are active members of the community, nor deny that the faith of the community is an important factor, it does not give full expression to the sacramental reality and ought to be discouraged.

Second-Class Christians?

The present practice of separating the sacraments of initiation when an infant is incorporated into the Christian community seems to imply that there are degrees of membership within the community—that baptism alone somehow makes one a second-class citizen of the community. Baptism and Eucharist form a sacramental continuum which is negated when the sacraments are separated. This is a reality of the Western Church to-day, yet a theological and pastoral anomaly just the same. The very lines drawn between sacramental praxis East and West only serve to compound the confusion and to multiply the questions.

In the Eastern churches infants are fully initiated, while in the Latin (Western) churches they are considered candidates for baptism alone and must achieve the use of reason (unless there is danger of death) before receiving Eucharist and confirmation.[21] Adults receive baptism and con-firmation before being welcomed to the Eucharist, but children baptized as infants usually receive Eucharist before confirmation. In the case of those children, we say they are not yet fully initiated, but what does that mean? How does the membership of an incompletely initiated nine-year-old differ from that of a fully initiated ten-year-old?

I realize that there are enough questions in the previous paragraph to keep an army of theologians busy for the rest of the century. I raise them here and will discuss them again in the following chapter, not to provide answers, but rather to subject pastoral practice to theological analysis. It is important for us as members of the believing community to see the connection (or lack of it) between belief and practice.

Agenda for the Future

With the official restoration of the catechumenate serving as a basis for the RCIA, discussions on infant baptism are surfacing more and more areas of catechumenal application.[22] In general such proposals fall into two cate-gories: those involved in pastoral practice suggest using the structure of the catechumenate for catechizing non-practicing parents who request bap-tism for their children,[23] whereas some theologians are more inclined to recommend incorporating infants and young children into the catechumenate.[24] Of the two proposals, however, the second appears to be a practice in search of a theology, since in the United States the pres-ent practice consists in baptizing infants, catechizing them for a short pe-riod of time when they reach an educable age, admitting them to Eucharist, catechizing them some more, and then expecting some sort of mature com-mitment before confirming them, when they are about twelve years of age. Practically speaking, therefore, these baptized children are, in prac-tice (but not in theology) baptized catechumens.[25]

This procedural difficulty is not unique to the Roman Catholic tradi-tion, but is common to those Christian traditions in which infant baptism is common practice. Writing in *The Baptism Quarterly*, George Rusling broadens our perspective on the issue:

> this indicates that [the baptized child's] relationship to the Church is that of a catechumen though it is a prolonged catechumenate. . . . The aim and purpose of the various ministries is nothing else but that of the catechumenate, for everything that is being done is in the hope of an eventual personal response. . . . The pastoral realities of the catechumenate are perfectly familiar to us. What we have to do is to make allowance for the idea of it in our theology of the Church.[26]

An African Solution?

The bishop of the diocese of Dapango in Togo sought Rome's advice with regard to a pastoral problem in his diocese.

Native tribesmen, with no intention of converting to Christianity, were bringing their children to the missionary priests to be baptized. The priests were troubled. They knew that they could not baptize the children because there was virtually no expectation that the children would be raised as Christians. At the same time, however, their missionary instinct was disturbed by making such a decision. The parents saw baptism as something that was good, and although they did not want it for themselves, like parents everywhere, they wanted the best for their children. The bishop presented this dilemma to the Congregation for the Doctrine of the Faith.

The solution proposed by Rome was that the missionaries be instructed to "inscribe the names" of these children.[27] It was reasoned that by doing so the parents' interests would be respected, while at the same time a connection would be made between the Church and the child. By virtue of that connection, missionaries might be more able to foster the relationship as the child grew.

Such a solution seems to be quite wise, but it raises for us another issue. An inscription of names is similar, if not identical, to the first ritual in the Rite of Christian Initiation of Adults and its adaptation for children of catechetical age (RCIC). Therefore, by recommending that their names be inscribed is the Sacred Congregation suggesting that these infants be regarded as catechumens? This could be the first step in a theology that addresses the pastoral reality of the Church today.

The theological ramifications of this solution are most dramatic and most important. If it were possible to enroll infants as catechumens, a workable option would be available so that faith could once again be the sole criteria for acceptance into the Christian community. Rather than

presuming some barely discernible type of faith, this means of incorporation would encourage a concrete transformation of the individual.[28] It
would be possible to administer the three sacraments of initiation together
when the individual was sufficiently prepared to become a member of the
community. This would not necessarily eliminate infant baptism, but it
would make adult initiation normative in the reality of common practice, rather than just ideologically, as it is at present.

To follow this line of thinking, as you might suspect, does not by any
means settle all related issues. In fact, some new ones arise related to what
motivates one to request incorporation into the Order of Catechumens.
Although catechumens, as we saw in chapter three, are not required to
make a profession of faith at the time of their enrollment in the Order
of Catechumens, they are asked to state what they want from the Church.[29]
Infants cannot do that any more than they can make a solemn profession
of faith, so we would still be tampering with the essential meaning of
sacramental structure to a certain degree.

Another theological implication raised by enrolling children in the
catechumenate, which is pointed out by Mark Searle, noting a "possible
inconsistency" between "subjecting the helpless infant to the 'sacramentality' of enrollment in the catechumenate, but refusing to submit it to
the 'sacramentality' of the complete rite of initiation."[30]

Peaceful Co-existence

If the Church did begin to enroll children in the order of catechumens,
could the two practices co-exist?

Practically speaking, they do co-exist—experientially if not
theologically—in the present-day Church. Children of the community's
active members, baptized because of their parents' profound faith-
commitment, are raised with the experience of seeing the faith lived:

> The Christian family is called to understand the events of its life—especially
> something as significant as pregnancy and childbirth—in the light of faith
> and to recognize the birth of each new child not only as a gift of God in
> some generic sense but as a specific word-event of God addressed to them.[31]

Children who were baptized solely as a social convention might never have
such an experience on an intimate level. In addition to actualizing theological integrity, advantages to the advent of such an alternative can be
seen on several different levels.

Pastorally, this development would allow for more flexibility. Indiscriminate infant baptism persists because there is no other pastoral al-

ternative. For this reason the weakest excuse for faith is deemed acceptable. Not all pastors are entirely comfortable with this decision they must make, and parents are often not prepared to make a serious faith-commitment in the name of their child, although they do want their child to grow as a member of the Christian community. With the possibility of a catechumenate, the decision of whether or not to have their child baptized could more realistically be returned to the parents. Children in the catechumenate would be able to have a more personal understanding of how the faith is lived by contact with members of the catechumenal community. At the time of their baptism they would be able to make an unencumbered decision of their own in a ritual which would give dramatic testimony to their commitment.

Sociologically, the community-dimension of the Church would be strengthened, for it is the community that is responsible for the growth of catechumenal faith. Unlike the pre-Vatican II Church, many of the present-day practices emphasize the communal dimension of the liturgy. The role of the family and the local ecclesial community is expressed both literally and symbolically in sacramental practices, as it has become increasingly more common for sacraments to be celebrated individually in a community setting. This would be more highly developed with a catechumenate, since the community would take an active part in the catechesis as well as in the celebration. Rather than focusing on the individual in isolation, this process would work towards creating a Christian environment within communities, as an end result of the conversion of individual members and their commitment to each other in faith.

Psychologically, the institution of such a catechumenate would remove the overwhelming and needless concern over infant damnation, which lingers as a mis-understanding of the concept of limbo. From the very earliest days of the Church catechumens have been considered to be members of the Christian community:

> as the catechumens have the sign of the cross on their forehead, they are already of the great house; but from servants let them become sons. For they are something who already belong to the great house.[32]   *Augustine*

The present rite also supports this understanding of the catechumens' place in the community:

> From this time on the Church embraces the catechumens as its own with a mother's love and concern. Joined to the Church, the catechumens are now part of the household of Christ, since the Church nourishes them with the word of God and sustains them by means of liturgical celebrations. The

catechumens should be eager, then, to take part in the celebrations of the word of God and to receive blessings and other sacramentals. When two catechumens marry or when a catechumen marries an unbaptized person, the appropriate rite is used. One who dies during the catechumenate receives a Christian burial.[33]

A catechumen, therefore, is neither a non-member nor a non-Christian, but a Christian *in fieri* and a member of both the local community and the universal Church.[34] This single fact would probably make the concept of a catechumenate most acceptable to the ecclesial community.

The Children's Catechumenate

A model for such a system already exists in the reality of pastoral practice. Infants baptized are later catechized through the Catholic school system or a CCD program. At some point they are called upon to re-affirm their commitment to the Church, usually in conjunction with reception of the sacrament of confirmation. It would not take a great deal of re-adjustment, therefore, to actualize a catechumenal process for children, and the RCIA even provides the rites for initiating children of catechetical age.[35]

A key question, I believe, is to ask whether or not as an ecclesial community we would pay more attention to the children if they were catechumens than we do now. I find a scandalous inconsistency when we baptize infants and then ignore them in our preaching and teaching until they reach school age, when the programs step in to help. But what happens when the community gathers for Eucharist? In my experience our celebrations are rarely geared to general audiences but more to adults only, which excludes a huge section of the baptized from more than receiving holy communion. These are serious questions that need our attention.

The implications of developing a children's catechumenate extend to the individual, the local community, and the universal Church. This development leaves room for the possibility of personal commitment celebrated in a communal setting at a later date. Although this has been viewed as an over-emphasis on the individual, it is precisely by means of this stress on the individualness of salvation, which is depicted in a splendid ceremonial, that the members of the community re-affirm their own commitment to Jesus. The corporate faith of the community is witnessed by the members' personal commitment to Jesus in response to God's prevenient grace. Simultaneously, the universal Church benefits from the renewal of individual communities. Therefore, it can be seen that through the visibility of the catechumenate which is basic to the RCIA, the possibility of including children within the structure emerges as worthy of consideration.

NOTES

1. Joachim Jeremias, *Infant Baptism in the First Four Centuries*, trans. David Cairns (Philadelphia: Westminster Press, 1962); *The Origins of Infant Baptism*, trans. Dorothea M. Barton, Studies in Historical Theology, vol. 1 (London: SCM Press, 1950).

2. Oscar Cullman, *Baptism in the New Testament*, trans. J.K.S. Reid, Studies in Biblical Theology, vol. 1 (London: SCM Press, 1950).

3. Acts 10:2; 11:4; 16:5, 31, 33; 18:8; John 4:53; 1 Cor 1:16.

4. Kurt Aland, *Did the Early Church Baptize Infants?* trans. G. R. Beasley-Murray (Philadelphia: Westminster Press, 1963).

5. Karl Barth, *The Teaching of the Church Regarding Baptism*, trans. E. Payne (London: SCM Press, 1948).

6. Although this has often been suggested by theologians of the Reformed traditions, Roman Catholics are also beginning to see this as a possibility. *See* Edward K. Braxton, "Adult Initiation and Infant Baptism," in *Becoming a Catholic Christian: A Symposium on Christian Initiation* (New York: Sadlier, 1978) 174–89; Paul F. X. Covino "The Postconciliar Infant Baptism Debate in the American Catholic Church," *Worship* 56 (1982) 240–60; G. W. Rusling, "The Status of Children," *Baptist Quarterly* 18 (1959–60) 245–57.

7. CSL, no. 67, 160.

8. *Rite of Baptism for Children* [RBC] (Washington: United States Catholic Conference, 1969) no. 5.

9. *Ibid.*

10. *RBC*, no. 8.4.

11. Mark Searle, "Infant Baptism Reconsidered," in *Alternative Futures for Worship*, vol. 2, *Baptism and Confirmation*, ed. Mark Searle (Collegeville: The Liturgical Press, 1987) 44.

12. *LG*, no. 9, 26.

13. Karl Rahner, *Theological Investigations* VII (London: Darton, Longman, and Todd, 1971) 92.

14. World Council of Churches, *One Lord, One Baptism: Study Report of the Faith and Order Commission* (London: SCM Press, 1961) 61.

15. Ralph Keifer, "Christian Initiation: The State of the Question," *Worship* 48 (1974) 397.

16. Christiane Brusselmans, "Christian Parents and Infant Baptism," *Louvain Studies* 2 (Spring 1968) 31.

17. Andrew Greeley, *Crisis in the Church: A Study of Religion in America* (Chicago: Thomas More Press, 1976) 193–212.

18. *Order of Christian Funerals*, no. 282 (Washington: International Commission on English in the Liturgy, 1985, 1989).

19. Christopher Kiesling, "Infant Baptism," *Worship* 42 (1968) 621. *See* Paul K. Jewett, *Infant Baptism and the Covenant of Grace* (Grand Rapids: Eerdmans, 1978).

20. *RBC*, no. 39.

21. CIC, 889.2.

22. *See* James B. Dunning, "The Rite of Christian Initiation of Adults: Model of Adult Growth," *Worship* 53 (1979) 142–57.

23. This is generally the way the problem has been handled in France. *See* Henri Holstein, "Le baptême des petits enfants," *Etudes* 324 (1966) 547–51.

24. *See* Charles Gusmer, "The Revised Adult Initiation and Its Challenge to Religious Education," *Living Light* 13 (1976) 92–98; Aidan Kavanagh, "Christian Initiation for Those Baptized as Infants," *Living Light* 13 (1976) 387–96.

25. *See* Jean-Philippe Bonnard, "Le temps du baptême: vers un catechumenat des enfants?" *Etudes* 333 (1970) 431–42.

26. Rusling, "The Status of Children" 247.

27. Pierre-Marie Gy, "Un document de la congregation pour la doctrine do la foi sure le bapteme des petits enfants," *La Maison-Dieu* 104 (1970) 101. *See also* Paul Vanbergen, "Baptism of the Infants of *non satis credentes* Parents," *Studia Liturgica* 12 (1977) 195–200.

28. Although baptism does have a reality apart from the faith of the individual, the structure would allow for more flexibility as to the time, manner, and quality of celebrating that reality.

29. RCIA, 50.

30. Searle, "Infant Baptism Reconsidered" 30.

31. *Ibid.* 35.

32. Augustine, *Tract on John* 11:4 (Edinburgh: Clark, 1873) 155.

33. RCIA, no. 47, 18.

34. Aidan Kavanagh, "The Norm of Baptism: The New Rite of Christian Initiation of Adults," *Worship* 48 (1974) 147.

35. RCIA, nos. 242–306. *See* Paul Philibert, "Children's Ritual Enculturation: What, How and Why?" *Catechumenate* 11 (March 1989) 27–44.

CHAPTER SIX

Confirmation

Debate concerning the sacrament of confirmation is neither new nor native to the Roman Catholic Church. Rather, Confirmation's history, theology, and pastoral practice have been studied and re-assessed time and again in the Roman Catholic and the Reformed traditions alike.[1] In contrast to the slight variation in the theology and practice of other sacraments, this aspect of confirmation is not only unique, but is also indicative of the vagueness of its sacramental practice. The questions are all familiar:

> How did confirmation come to be a separate sacrament?
> Does confirmation have a theological significance distinct from baptism?
> At what age should one receive the sacrament of confirmation?

The questions continue to be debated, but definite answers are not found.[2] It is possible, however, to organize the proposed answers in such a way that the areas of difficulty emerge from the morass of questions. When we examine these issues in the light of the whole process of Christian initiation, we can see the relationship between them and the implementation of the RCIA quite dramatically, for the RCIA's implementation establishes a firm understanding of confirmation's place in the initiation continuum.

This approach to confirmation will demonstrate that:

1. Historical data show that confirmation is the result of an evolutionary process, and only in that context can it be properly understood.
2. The theological significance of confirmation is directly related to the theological significance of baptism.
3. In pastoral practice confirmation is used to answer a variety of pastoral needs.

Historical Data

There is no unambiguous evidence of a separate sacrament of confirmation in the New Testament, although numerous references to the Holy Spirit have been traditionally cited as such—the inevitable result of redaction criticism as scholars search for scriptural documentation for later liturgical practice. Tracing the history of confirmation ultimately leads back to baptism, for what are now termed the separate sacraments of baptism and confirmation were historically two moments in the process of Christian initiation.[3]

When the early Christian communities came to incorporate new members sacramentally, they symbolically reproduced those two events upon which the foundation of the Church hinged—the death/resurrection of Jesus and the advent of the Holy Spirit. While these were historically separate events, in the Church they became one, for in standing apart from the events the community could see them as part of the providential dynamism of the Father. This was, in turn, manifested liturgically, within the single ritual of Christian initiation, as two symbolic actions expressing the christological and pneumatological aspects of the Church, and leading to the celebration of them in the Eucharist. Rather than signifying the giving of the Spirit, then, the second rite referred instead back to the gift of the Spirit at baptism by recalling the historical event and its importance for the Church.[4] The Holy Spirit was received in the baptismal bath, and symbolically expressed in the anointing and laying on of hands.

While this pattern of initiation remained constant in the Eastern Church, by the fifth century it had begun to be altered radically in the Western Church, as the two moments in the initiation process became separated.[5] This alteration appears to have been the direct result of two developments: the atrophy of the catechumenate, and the continuation of episcopal domination over the ministry of confirmation. Neither of these causes flows from a re-examination or re-interpretation of the theology of confirmation, but rather both are external cultural factors that have affected our present-day understanding of the sacrament of confirmation.

As infant baptism came to be increasingly widespread, the Church ceased to be primarily a missionary enterprise, with the result that the catechumenate began to atrophy.[6] Since the Church had grown dramatically by that time, *chorepiscopoi* and presbyters had assumed the jurisdiction of local churches. Unlike the bishops of the East who passed along the privilege of confirming to the minister of baptism, however, the bishops of the West reserved this privilege to themselves, which led to the separation of the sacraments of initiation. Once separated, the time-gap between them continued to increase gradually, which led to a shift in the theological significance of the rite as well.[7]

Theological Significance

The first error that tends to be made in discussions concerning the sacraments of baptism and confirmation is that they are treated as isolated actions, completed when each ritual is over. In reality, together they mark the beginning of a process which must continue to develop and to be realized in the Church. In order to be theologically intelligible, both sacraments must be understood as parts of a single process of initiation. Confirmation, therefore, is intrinsically related to baptism, and in isolation is not essentially constitutive of membership in the community.[8]

St. Thomas Aquinas[9] set to rest the issue of confirmation's sacramentality, and his theological explanation[10] of confirmation prevailed during the ensuing centuries, but during the Reformation theologians sought to ground his explanation more firmly in Scripture.[11] That attempt led to wholesale appropriation of any mention of the coming of the Holy Spirit in the New Testament, giving an erroneous picture of the scriptural roots for a later interpretation of the sacrament of confirmation.[12]

The further away confirmation moved from baptism temporally, the further it moved theologically until it eventually became enmeshed with a concept of maturity completely foreign to its origin. In the twentieth century this notion of maturity as a pre-requisite for the reception of the sacrament of confirmation was even further compounded.

Before Pius X's decree *Quam Singulari* in 1910, children in the United States were confirmed prior to receiving first Eucharist. Canon Law (1917) stipulated that a child should receive confirmation at approximately age seven[13] following a period of catechetical instruction.[14] When Pius X advocated that children receive communion at an earlier age, however, a leap-frog effect was seen in the sacraments of initiation, and confirmation was left behind as communion moved into its place sequentially. This only served to intensify the association of confirmation with maturity.

In 1940 Pius XII issued a decree which stated it was the right and duty of priests to confer the sacrament of confirmation in case of necessity.[15] This marked the first change in the episcopal domination of the sacrament, and thus allowed the possibility of uniting baptism and confirmation if only in the unusual and dire circumstances it cited. This necessity of reintegrating the sacraments of initiation was further developed in the documents of Vatican II:

> The rite of confirmation is to be revised and the intimate connection which this sacrament has with the whole of Christian initiation is to be more lucidly set forth.[16]

The apostolic constitution *Divinae Consortium Naturae*, issued by Paul VI on August 15, 1971, reiterated the Council's aim and went one step further in emphasizing that the connection between the sacraments of initiation should not only be demonstrated by their association, but should also be evident in the rite and words by which confirmation is conferred. Along with the new rite, therefore, a new formula was included, and today the sacrament of confirmation is conferred through the anointing with chrism on the forehead, which is done by the laying on of the hand, and through the words: "Be sealed with the Gift of the Holy Spirit."[17]

Thus, shifts in emphasis amount to a good beginning, but they do not constitute the whole answer because maturity continues to be a dominant theme in the literature concerning confirmation, resulting in serious difficulties for theologians—difficulties which have yet to be satisfactorily remedied.

Today's Difficulties

The first difficulties arise with the concept of maturity itself. It is too ambiguous a concept, for maturation is a multi-dimensional process which is subject to innumerable variables. Therefore, just as it is difficult to find the proper barometer of faith necessary to justify infant baptism, it is likewise difficult to find an adequate measure of maturity in order to establish the proper age for confirmation. Is one to be concerned with chronological age or spiritual maturity? To set chronological age as a standard might appear to be ludicrous, but attempts to ascertain spiritual maturity would probably be even less valid.

Secondly, when maturity becomes a pre-requisite for confirmation, the sacrament's relationship with baptism becomes obscured. Consequently, it denies confirmation the theological ground from which it evolved and imposes instead a dimension to the sacrament which cannot be justified historically, theologically, or liturgically. The result of all this is that we link God's grace to the physical maturation process, so that when one reaches a particular chronological age, one is able to receive the grace of confirmation.

Thirdly, such a link between confirmation and maturity is not supported by the rite itself. The bishop and priests who minister the sacrament lay hands on the candidates and say:

> All-powerful God, Father of our Lord Jesus Christ,
> by water and the Holy Spirit
> you freed your sons and daughters from sin
> and gave them new life.
> Send your Holy Spirit upon them
> to be their Helper and Guide.
> Give them the spirit of wisdom and understanding,
> the spirit of right judgment and courage,
> the spirit of knowledge and reverence.
> Fill them with the spirit of wonder and awe in your presence.
> We ask this through Christ our Lord.[18]

All of the prayers and instructions speak of confirmation as a completion of baptism. The rite takes place in the context of the Liturgy of the Eucharist "to express more clearly the fundamental connection of this sacrament with the entirety of Christian initiation."[19] In a startling move, the Rite of Confirmation abrogated canon 796.1,[20] and indicated it was desirable for the godparent at baptism also to serve as sponsor at confirmation to express more clearly the relationship between the sacraments.[21] The Rite of Confirmation itself also establishes a connection. After the homily the candidates renew their baptismal promises, which is followed by the laying on of hands and the sacramental chrismation.[22]

The sacrament of confirmation symbolically expresses the gift of the Spirit that was received in baptism. No element of the rite supports the celebration of confirmation as a sacrament of maturity, but pastoral practice indicates that it continues to be envisioned as such.

Pastoral Practice

Each semester when I begin studying the sacrament of confirmation with my liturgy class at the university, I use an exercise which I refer to as collecting our experience. I ask the students to think back to the time of their confirmation and to recall what it meant to them. Once they have briefly recorded that experience, I ask them to list the details of the experience—what they wore, what name they chose, who their sponsor was, what the requirements were for sponsors, what symbols were used, who administered the sacrament, and any other details they might consider relevant. Then we collect the experience.

What emerges from our collection is a potpourri—confirmation practice in the New York metropolitan area a decade ago. The students are shocked, because they thought that their corner of the experience was the generic confirmation. It never entered their minds that experiences could be so different.

Over the years these collections have generally shown that the dominant practice in our area is to confirm young people between the ages of ten and eighteen. Increasingly, eligibility for reception of the sacrament has involved not only participation in a preparation program, but also the completion of some type of community service project. (Ironically, this reminds me of the required hours of community service one needs to accumulate before being considered a proper debutante.)

The attire for confirmation these days is quite wide-ranging, with white or red choir robes heading the list. Where robes are used, it is often customary to dress the boys and girls in different colors, further complicating an already complicated sacramental practice. Stoles were added a few years ago, and many parishes seem to have leapt onto that bandwagon, decorating the stoles with doves and confirmation names, without ever taking into consideration the fact that they were misusing our symbol for priesthood, further muddying the confirmation waters.

An obvious symbol for confirmation that rarely seems to be used is the baptismal candle. In the last seven years, only one student out of the close to 1500 that I have taught in this course ever recorded such a use of the candle as a symbol of the light of faith they were given in baptism.

When we begin discussing sponsors, the students really begin to seem hostile as they share their recollections. Apparently their feelings were often hurt in the process of choosing a sponsor. The person they wanted was not eligible for consideration for what they now learn to be the most arbitrary of reasons. Many had to have a parent as sponsor, while others were forbidden to have their parents involved.[23] Some were encouraged to choose their godparents, but none seemed to recall selecting a person on the basis of their witness to Christianity.

They were most excited about finally selecting a name of their own, and that was generally their starting point—a name they liked rather than a saint whom they wanted to accept as a model. Few students were asked to consider using their baptismal names, and those who were encouraged to do so often selected their baptismal patron.

To the question regarding other memories the answers were somewhat surprising. They remember parties and gifts, and being disappointed. With all of the preparations that went into the process, they expected to feel differently after being confirmed, or at the very least to be treated differently as members of the community. Once confirmed they thought they could be lectors or Eucharistic ministers, only to be told they had to wait until they were eighteen. Many thought it a cruel hoax to let them think they were making an adult commitment and then be treated like children again.

All of these practices perpetuate a faulty understanding of the theological significance of the sacrament of confirmation. There is nothing in the liturgical rite to support using confirmation as a Christian Bar Mitzvah. When we allow for such a dichotomy between what we celebrate and what we prepare young people to celebrate, we ought not to be surprised at their disappointment. What our practice seems to be saying is that for those baptized as infants, we need some ritual re-affirmation of faith at a later stage of life. To force confirmation to fulfill that purpose is detrimental to its original meaning.

Theologians Respond

Some theologians and catechists, for a considerable time now, have advocated moving confirmation back to infancy in the case of infant baptism.[24] Their position is based on the belief that no more maturity is necessary for confirmation than for baptism. While the result of this shift would be to effect a more historically-sound and theologically-acceptable celebration, it would still not address the pastoral demand for a mature re-affirmation of faith. Instead, it would perpetuate the problems already inherent in infant baptism, and there would still be a need to develop some type of ritual for re-affirmation of faith as members approached adulthood.

A practice that seems to be gaining more momentum in recent days is that of restoring the order of the sacraments of initiation by celebrating the sacrament of confirmation when the child reaches the age of discretion, either in a single celebration linked with the reception of Eucharist, or the year prior to the child's first reception of Eucharist. Several large-scale diocesan projects with this type of implementation are described in detail in the recent book *When Should We Confirm?*[25] Although such a program in itself still does not respond to the need for some ritual affirmation of faith at a more mature age, the dioceses that are involved in these projects are also in the process of developing some type of diocesan celebration of the ritual passage from adolescence to adulthood. The Diocese of Salford (England), for example, intends to have such a ritual coincide with leaving secondary school.[26]

Another popular catechetical strain envisions the rite of confirmation as a form of lay ordination.[27] While it is true that many of the ritual elements in confirmation parallel those of holy orders (laying on of hands, consignation, chrismation), that is because both confirmation and holy orders derive this symbolism from the sacrament of baptism. Baptism is the sacrament that ordains us to priesthood; that dimension is recalled in confirmation, but given sacerdotal function through holy orders.

Confirmation Tomorrow

It is not only inconsistent, but also pedagogically unsound to have two different theological understandings of the same sacrament—one for infants and another for adults (or children of catechetical age as mandated by the RCIA). Catechetical questions concerning the theology and pastoral practice of confirmation are serious ones, but they are more properly questions concerning ecclesial life than sacramental practice. Each sacrament must be seen in the context of the life of the Church, and each sacrament of initiation must be seen in the light of the totality of the initiation process. Consequently, what is involved in the resolution of these issues is not revision of confirmation practice, but renewal of the initiation process. Such a renewal, we know, is afforded the Church in the RCIA.

The model of initiation presented in the RCIA re-establishes the baptism-confirmation-Eucharist continuum as the norm of sacramental initiation—a necessary step in recovering the original meaning of confirmation. Theologically and liturgically, Eucharist is the climax of the initiation process, as *Presbyterorum Ordinis* indicates:

> Hence the Eucharist shows itself to be the source and the apex of the whole work of preaching the gospel. Those under instruction are introduced by stages to a sharing in the Eucharist. The faithful, already marked with the sacred seal of baptism and confirmation, are through the reception of the Eucharist fully joined to the Body of Christ.[28]

As long as individuals continue to receive the Eucharist before they are confirmed, a theologically-sound understanding of confirmation as it is presently celebrated in the Rite of Confirmation will be difficult to affirm by pastoral practice.

A further step in recovering the original meaning of confirmation is taken by the RCIA in allowing the minister of baptism to confirm the neophyte.[29] The document is very clear on the reason for this alteration:

In accord with the ancient practice followed in the Roman liturgy, adults are not to be baptized without receiving confirmation immediately afterward, unless some serious reason stands in the way. The conjunction of the two celebrations signifies the unity of the paschal mystery, the close link between the mission of the Son and outpouring of the Holy Spirit, and the connection between the two sacraments through which the Son and the Holy Spirit come with the Father to those who are baptized.[30]

It would follow, then, that if the baptizing presbyter could confirm an adult for the sake of theological and sacramental integrity, he could also confirm an infant for the same reasons. The RCIA, therefore, provides the model for renewing the initiation process necessary for a proper approach to confirmation.

NOTES

1. *See Crisis for Confirmation,* ed. Michael Perry (London: SCM Press, 1967). Canon Perry's study examines the debate within the Anglican Church, with reference to the other Reformed traditions as well. *See also When Should We Confirm?,* ed. James A. Wilde (Chicago: Liturgy Training Publications, 1989). In contrast, this collection of articles provides us with recent approaches to the sacrament of confirmation within the Roman Catholic communion.

2. Gerard Austin, *The Rite of Confirmation: Anointing with the Spirit* (New York: Pueblo, 1985); Aidan Kavanagh, "Confirmation: A Suggestion from Structure," *Worship* 58 (1984) 386–95; *Confirmation: Origins and Reform* (New York: Pueblo, 1988); Thomas Marsh, *A Gift of Community: Baptism and Confirmation* (Wilmington: Michael Glazier, 1985).

3. *See* Thomas Marsh, "A Study of Confirmation," *Irish Theological Quarterly* 39 (1972) 149–63; 319–36; 40 (1973) 125–47; "The Theology of Confirmation," *Furrow* 27 (1976) 606–16; Hans Kung, "What is Confirmation?" in *Signposts of the Future: Contemporary Issues Facing the Church* (New York: Doubleday, 1978) 178–203.

4. Marsh, "A Study of Confirmation," *Irish Theological Quarterly* 40 (1973) 140–46.

5. *See* Nathan Mitchell, "Dissolution of the Rite of Christian Initiation," in *Made Not Born: New Perspectives on Christian Initiation and the Catechumenate,* ed. Murphy Center for Liturgical Research (Notre Dame: University of Notre Dame Press, 1976) 50–82.

6. While one could maintain that the catechumenate died, liturgical scholars are beginning to see that the catechumenate actually migrated from the local community into religious houses and seminaries where it continued to exist as religious formation under modified conditions. *See also* John A. Bersten, "Christian Affections and the Catechumenate," *Worship* 52 (1978) 194–210; C. Bouchard, "Journey of Faith: Initial Religious Formation as an Extension of the New Rite of Initiation of Adults," *Review for Religious* 36 (1977) 592–99.

7. *See* Mitchell, "Dissolution of the Rite of Christian Initiation," 66–69.

8. "Community" in this context is used with reference to the Christian community in general, and not limited to the Roman Catholic communion, which is obvious from present liturgical practice. Confirmation is administered in the Rite of Reception of Baptized Christians into Full Communion of the Catholic Church to those candidates who were not previously confirmed. The exception noted would be for members of Eastern Orthodox Churches which maintain the integrity of the initiation sacraments. RCIA, nos. 493–94.

9. St. Thomas Aquinas is not the only scholastic theologian who expounded on the subject of confirmation, but his work is traditionally cited as typifying the theological understanding of his time. See Summa Theologicae III, q. 72 (Rome: Marietti, 1956).

10. Although he first cited the institution of confirmation as occurring when Jesus laid hands upon the children in Matt 19:15 (Scriptum Super Sententiis IV, Distinction VII, "De Confirmatione" (Paris: Lethielleux, 1947), he later altered his explanation (Summa Theologicae III, q. 72, a. 1, ad. 1) by asserting that Jesus did institute the sacrament directly, but by means of promise (John 16:7). To explain this anomaly, he noted that the Spirit could not have been given before the Lord's resurrection and ascension. For Thomas the chrismation was the essential form of the sacrament and reflected the tradition that the laying on of hands was contained in the anointing. He also emphasized the necessity of the words, "I sign thee with the sign of the cross and confirm thee with the chrism of salvation," (q. 72, a. 3).

11. Both Cranmer and Bucer, for example, found a scriptural basis to justify and to encourage both infant baptism and confirmation, with which Calvin took issue. See J.D.C. Fisher, Christian Initiation: The Reformation Period (London: SPCK, 1970); Leonel L. Mitchell, "Christian Initiation: The Reformation Period," in Made Not Born, 83–98.

12. See J.D.C. Fisher, Confirmation Then and Now (London: SPCK, 1978) 139–41.

13. CIC (1917), Canon 788. This canon also allowed for earlier administration if the child was in danger of death or if some other grave reason should necessitate it.

14. CIC (1917), Canon 786.

15. AAS 38 (1946) 349–54.

16. SC, no. 71.

17. Rite of Confirmation [RC] (Washington: United States Catholic Conference, 1975) no. 9.

18. RC, no. 25.

19. RC, no. 13.

20. CIC (1917), Canon 796.1. "One must be different from the baptismal sponsor, unless there be a plausible reason to disregard this rule, or confirmation is legitimately administered after baptism."

21. RC, no. 5.

22. There was some debate initially concerning the sacramental symbolism of this rite, for some theologians saw the laying on of hands as the proper form of the sacrament. See Gerald Austin, "What Has Happened to Confirmation?" Worship 50 (1976) 420–26.

23. As of 1983 the revised Code of Canon Law has clarified this point, by stating that the requirements for a confirmation sponsor are the same as those of a baptism sponsor. CIC Canons 893 and 874.1.

24. Richard Ling, "A Catechists Vote for Infant Confirmation," Living Light 7 (1970) 42–56.

25. Wilde, When Should We Confirm?

26. Ibid. 44–45.

27. See John Cardinal Wright, "Some Reflections on Confirmation," L'Osservatore Romano 22 (June 1, 1978) 9–10.

28. PO, no. 5.

29. RCIA, no. 232.

30. RCIA, no. 215.

CHAPTER SEVEN

Penance: An Endangered Species?

Have you begun to wonder lately whether or not the sacrament of reconciliation is on the verge of extinction? Surely, when we compare sacramental practice today with that we knew a generation ago, it is obvious that a drastic change has taken place. In 1972, Francis Buckley, S.J., wrote, "During the last few years there has been a sharp drop in confession: about 50 percent in Europe and up to 75 percent in some parts of the United States."[1] If that was the state of affairs seventeen years ago, what would those statistics be today? At a recent meeting between Vatican officials and United States Bishops, Archbishop Kucera referred to a survey conducted by the Bishops' Committee on Pastoral Research and Practices which states that "25 percent of practicing Catholics receive the sacrament of penance weekly, monthly or every other month. Slightly more than half . . . receive the sacrament once or twice a year. But 19 percent . . . report that they no longer have recourse to this sacrament."[2] The truth is obvious: people are simply not availing themselves of the sacrament of reconciliation to the same degree they once were.

How well I remember Saturday after Saturday, anxiously waiting on those endless lines for a tense two minutes in the darkened confessional with a shadow-masked priest. Gone is the *angst,* gone are the confessional queues, and Saturdays now find church buildings deserted.

Where are all those people today?

Has everyone stopped sinning?

Has the sacrament of reconciliation become an endangered species?

What effect can the RCIA have on the sacramental practice of reconciliation?

Surely there is evidence of concern on all levels, as a list of recent articles and pronouncements will indicate.[3] The problem is multi-faceted and very deeply rooted among us. Therefore more is required than issuing a directive that Catholics get back in the confession queue, as will be discussed in this chapter. However, we must begin by surveying the scene to grasp the dimensions of the danger posed for this sacrament.

Surveying the Scene

In my work as a university professor, trying to educate and prepare young men and women for their role in the Church of tomorrow, I have given much attention to the pastoral situation of sacramental reconciliation today. That has led me to many parish settings where I have presented workshops on the sacrament of reconciliation, both for general audiences and for the parents of children preparing for first Eucharist. In working with adults preparing for entrance into full communion with the Roman Catholic Church, I have also had the privilege of participating in the process of catechesis. Each of these three groups has a different agenda, one might say, but the core issues remain the same: fear, confusion, and discomfort.

For seven years now at the university, I have been teaching a course entitled "The Liturgy Today." In addition to covering the history of the liturgy, the course incorporates basic sacramental theology. It never fails that penance arouses keen interest in the students. Eagerly they tell their stories and touch once again their early fears. Some admit to having been yelled at by a priest, or even thrown out of the confessional for not being serious enough. Many own up to having fabricated sins in order to have something to confess, and everyone admits at least to having conjured up the numbers that accompanied the offenses. In recounting these tales, their icy, age-old fears start to melt, and we can begin to look more honestly at the sacrament of reconciliation.

In the early 1970s, certain dioceses of the United States began experiments with deferring children's first confessions, allowing them to receive first Communion without prior reception of the sacrament of penance. Throughout the years of discussion, the Holy See continued to reaffirm the teaching of *Quam Singulari* (1910), placing first confession before first Communion, but Paul VI was willing to enter into dialogue with any conference of bishops that wanted to continue such experiments for a longer period of time.[4] Although permission for such experiments expired in 1973, various parishes throughout the country continued the practice of admitting children to first Eucharist without prior reception of the sacrament of reconciliation.

The children who were the subjects of those experiments are now reaching adulthood, making a detailed evaluation of the experiments possible for the first time. Within that age-group, however, are also many young men and women who are reaching adulthood without ever having received the sacrament of reconciliation or completed the sacraments of initiation. Their parents only enrolled them in parish religious education for a short time, and once they received their first Communion, they were not seen again. I expect we will see growing numbers of such young people over the next few years.

While actual experiences of sacramental reconciliation in a communal setting are more common today, many Catholics, particularly those who receive the sacrament weekly or monthly, have not experienced the communal forms of the sacrament. We must remember, however, that although the reformed Rite of Penance was promulgated in 1973, its implementation was not mandatory in the United States until the First Sunday of Lent 1977. Consequently, most people in the Church today were catechized for the sacrament under the discipline of the old ritual. Although some parishes began to celebrate the sacrament communally even before the new Rite of Penance was fully implemented, the opposite was more often the case, and in many parts of the country presbyters who continue to use the old form of the sacrament find the reformed rite too cumbersome.

Of all the stories about first confession that were told in class, however, one stood out far beyond the rest. One young woman told us that she had attended public school and participated in the parish CCD program sporadically, and then only until she received her first Communion. After that, with little or no encouragement from her parents to continue, she abandoned CCD classes completely, rarely even attended Mass. When she was eighteen and a senior in high school, however, one of her friends encouraged her to participate in a Christian Awakening weekend. Reluctantly she agreed, only to be stunned when Friday night's activities turned out to include a communal penance service. She was fearful, not at the prospect of confessing her sins, but because she was not sure of either what she should do or what was expected of her. She decided it would be better for her to sit back and observe for a while, as she thought over what might be her sins.

Six priests were hearing confessions in the front of the chapel. They looked like kind men to her, and she noticed the way they warmly greeted each penitent who approached them. The confession seemed so calm and the laying on of hands so powerful, that Pam longed to be a part of the experience. Still she held back, not knowing what to say or do. Finally unable to contain herself any longer, she hesitantly approached one of the priests. When Father Joe put his arm around her shoulder, though, a great peace descended upon her.

"I felt so comfortable, and right away I told Father Joe that this was my first confession. He helped me to talk about sin and the other things that were bothering me in life as well. When I felt his hands on my head in absolution, I knew that I was being embraced by the forgiving love of God."

By the time Pam had finished relating her experience, the entire class sat transfixed at the humble simplicity of her story. There was no sound, but I could see that Pam's words had conveyed an awesome sense of God's presence that few of her classmates had ever experienced. Most impressed, it seemed, were the seven students who had never received first penance.

It was Pam's experience in particular that caused me to do some serious theological reflection on the state of the sacrament of reconciliation today. Because I recognize reconciliation to have great value as a sacramental healing, I do not want it to be lost or relegated to a dark corner of ecclesiastical obscurity. Penance has spent too much time in the dark already!

In *Megatrends,* John Naisbitt introduces his readers to the "high tech/high touch" formula, which posits that the higher our technology becomes, the greater is our need for a counterbalancing human response.[5] It is immediately obvious to people with a good pastoral sense that in the sacrament of penance we have the possibility of a high touch sacrament at a deeply spiritual level. Following that principle, and given the technological intensity that pervades our world, it would seem that our need for the sacrament of penance today is even greater than it was a generation ago. That will be the context for my conclusions and recommendations.

Conclusions

In the 1960s, when Saturday confession lines began to disappear, it was not because people had stopped sinning or had decided to become scofflaws. No one gave us permission to stop going to confession; we just did. Society was changing, our image of God was changing, and these radically affected our previously un-questioned patterns of confessing sin.

Technology, by way of sophisticated satellite communications, had moved the world right into our homes overnight. Rather than having

Movietone News summarize world events for us, we had the Vietnam War fought in our living rooms. We walked on the moon with Neil Armstrong, and more recently sat stunned as *Challenger* exploded before our eyes. No longer are we shielded, even for an hour, from either the triumph or the suffering of the human community.[6] In the face of all this, it is not surprising that the Saturday ritual of confessing the same sins week after week would begin to seem meaningless—an immature hold-over from a previous era. For some, this led to latent conscience maturation; for others, to continued confusion about what actually constitutes sin.[7]

This phenomenon was accompanied by our changing concept of God. Perhaps it was high technology that began to transform God from a pseudo-benevolent despot to a loving parent in the 1960s, but I prefer to view it as a result of our beginning to celebrate Eucharist in our native tongue. Once we began to ponder our sinfulness in the penitential rite, to pray the Lord's Prayer in common, and to exchange the kiss of peace, we became more aware of other meaningful ways in which we are reconciled with God and with one another.

The *Baltimore Catechism* taught that the sacrament of penance was necessary only for the forgiveness of mortal sins. Venial sins, we learned, could be forgiven in other ways, in particular through devout reception of Eucharist. Yet, week after week we lined up to confess the same list of venial sins, just to be sure that they were forgiven, or perhaps to get extra grace. Today, before approaching the altar to receive Eucharist, as with one voice the assembly faithfully prays, "Lord, I am not worthy to receive you. Speak but the word, and I shall be healed." "*Domine non sum dignus, ut intres sub tectum meum, sed tantum dic verbo et sanabitur anima mea*" just doesn't have the same ring to it. Now we believe, and experience God's loving mercy more confidently.

Another reality of this age of technology is that therapy, spiritual direction, and specialized support groups now fill a need that was once met by periodic confession.[8] This trend, which began in the early 1970s when pop-psychology books began to hit the top of literary best-seller lists with increasing regularity, continues strongly today. Rather than being viewed negatively, however, in this development we ought to be able to recognize the beginnings of collective maturation and healthy conscience-formation. Such a trend will not threaten the sacrament of reconciliation, but has the possibility of helping to restore it to full vigor.[9] Toward that end, I make some specific recommendations.

Recommendations

1. *Begin to take SIN more seriously once again.*

In the past twenty years the people of God have not stopped sinning. In fact, along with the rest of our lives, our ways of sinning have often become more sophisticated as well. Pop psychology has helped us to see that much of what we used to consider sin (anger, jealousy, lust, for example) is more accurately defined as healthy emotional response to given stimuli.[10] When we allow that emotional response to affect our relationships, both with God and others, however, we have moved into the arena of sin. Although we might never have committed a single mortal sin, it does not mean that sin has never entered our hearts. Good preaching on the potential deadliness of sin would be a good first step to insuring the survival of the sacramental reconciliation.

2. *Distinguish between confession and reconciliation.*

Lumen Gentium refers to the Church as a sacrament of reconciliation—an instrument for achieving unity with God and the unity of the human family.[11] Confession of sins is but one moment in the process of sacramental reconciliation, which forms but a small part of the Church's ministry of reconciliation:

> The people of God accomplishes and perfects this continued repentence in many different ways. It shares in the suffering of Christ by enduring its own difficulties, carries out works of mercy and charity, and adopts ever more fully the outlook of the Gospel message. Thus the people of God becomes in the world a sign of conversion to God.[12]

Past fixation on the confession of sins blinded us to the process of reconciliation. The perceived meaninglessness of our old patterns of confession have been addressed in the revised ritual, but full implementation still awaits solid catechesis on reconciliation, and its place in our lives today.[13]

3. *Support and encourage penitential discipline.*

Prayer, fasting, and almsgiving, traditional penitential practices, need to be dusted off and put back into practice in our lives. Early Christians, recognizing their human frailty, used such forms of discipline to help them keep on the right road. The vestigial penances we were given in the confessional, most notably the proverbial three Hail Marys, hardly had the same impact. Friday abstinence and Lenten fasting unfortunately lost their penitential character over the years, becoming instead sort of club rules.

It is arrogant for us to think that we can walk in God's ways without God's help. Once upon a time many people thought that salvation lay in making the nine first Fridays and the five first Saturdays—the days when we were mired in minimalism. We hope that those days have come to an end!

Good confessors and inspired preachers could go a long way toward helping people look to God for strength and encouragement. With their help, instead of regarding penance as punishment, we might begin to recognize its medicinal value. To the frustrated mother who confesses her impatience and repeated outbursts of anger, a confessor might suggest praying Psalm 23, not to be prayed just once as a penance/punishment, but whenever those feelings of exasperation begin to mount, as a penance/discipline.[14]

4. *Recognize the continuum of baptism-Eucharist-penance.*

It is surprising when we study the history of the sacrament of penance to note its rather late development. Canonical or public penance, didn't emerge in the Church's practice until the third century. Prior to that time, the Church did not allow for the reconciliation of sinners after baptism. Private individual confession as we know it didn't gain official Church approval until the Fourth Lateran Council in 1215.

When we look to the ministry of Jesus, and compare that with the early Church's apparent refusal to readmit sinners, it seems as though the apostles' successors were violating an essential principle of Jesus' life and work. We must remember, however, that becoming a Christian in the early centuries was a much more involved process, and only followed upon three or four years of intensive preparation. Although the Rite of Penance might not have existed, *per se*, the Church certainly did allow for reconciliation of sinners. The sacrament of reconciliation in those days, however, was baptism.

There was also a greater appreciation in the early days of Christianity for the Eucharist as a sacrament of reconciliation. While canonical penance, from the third century on, was a method for reconciling those guilty of grave sin, the general Christian population was reconciled to God and to the community during the Eucharistic meal. The penitential rite was an element that appeared in Eucharistic celebrations as early as the second century.[15]

To recognize that both baptism and Eucharist are also sacraments of reconciliation will not rob the Rite of Penance of its place in the life of the Church. Rather, it will restore to sacramental reconciliation its proper place in the sacramental continuum.

5. *Discover ways to CELEBRATE reconciliation.*

Last semester a few students described their experiences with communal celebrations of reconciliation. Generally those celebrations occurred during a retreat or as part of their high school religion program. Not one student had ever participated in a parish celebration of the Rite of Penance.

Are we being honest with our children when we introduce them to sacramental reconciliation in a carefully crafted, liturgically-uplifting celebration? Will they ever encounter such a celebration again? Perhaps they will only find what I did last Advent.

The Sunday bulletin announced a "Communal Penance Service" for Wednesday evening at 8 p.m., which I decided to attend. As I arrived at the church that night, the 7:30 p.m. Mass was just ending and the people were leaving quickly. At 8 p.m., one of the priests came into the sanctuary and plugged in a tape recorder. Before turning it on, he announced to the dozen or so people present where each priest would be hearing confessions, and then left us to the music and the mercy of God. Apart from the music, and the short line, I felt as though a time machine had hurled me back to 1960.

When an identical announcement appeared during Lent, I optimistically attended again. The only difference, however, was that this time there was no music!

I know both from studying the ritual and from personal experience what wonderful possibilities there are for celebrations of reconciliation using the Rite of Penance. Some parishes celebrate reconciliation communally several times a year. One local parish has a celebration, worthy of particular note, during the annual parish celebration triduum of the Immaculate Conception. At least twenty priests from around the diocese are invited to serve as confessors for the occasion. They are carefully selected for their pastoral sensitivities, and their names are published in the parish bulletin the previous week, along with a note encouraging people to attend the celebration. Attend and celebrate they do, in a festival worthy of the wonder that is reconciliation with God and the community.

Such celebrations should make headlines in our diocesan papers, so that people will know that the Rite of Penace has a new lease on life in many parishes.[16]

Many more recommendations could be made, and perhaps in the coming years we will see them lived out in local communities. The bottom line is not how to make sin, penance, and reconciliation relevant today, but rather to allow their inherent relevance to be acknowledged and celebrated in our time.

NOTES

1. Francis J. Buckley, *"I Confess": The Sacrament of Penance Today* (Notre Dame: Ave Maria, 1972) 21.

2. Archbishop Kucera, "Liturgy and the Sacraments," *Origins* 18 (March 23, 1989) 696.

3. See *Reconciliation: The Continuing Agenda,* ed. Robert J. Kennedy (Collegeville: The Liturgical Press, 1987).

4. Pope Paul VI, Addendum to the *General Catechetical Directory,* dated March 18, 1971, as found in *Documents on the Liturgy 1963-79* (Collegeville: The Liturgical Press, 1982) 367-68. *See also* John Huels *Disputed Questions in the Liturgy Today* (Chicago: Liturgy Training Publications, 1988) 67-75.

5. Naisbitt, *Megatrends* 35-52.

6. Naisbitt refers to this as the demise of the "information float," *Ibid.* 14-19.

7. *See* Richard M. Gula, *To Walk Together Again: The Sacrament of Reconciliation* (New York: Paulist Press, 1984) 89-136.

8. *See* Kenneth Leech, *Soul Friend* (San Francisco: Harper and Row, 1980) 194-225.

9. Karl Rahner, "Problems Concerning Confession," *Theological Investigations,* III (Baltimore: Helicon Press, 1968) 205.

10. *See* John W. Glaser, "Conscience and Super-ego: A Key Distinction," *Theological Studies* 32 (1971) 30-47.

11. *Lumen Gentium* 1.1.

12. *Rite of Penance,* no. 4, as found in *The Rites of the Catholic Church* I (New York: Pueblo, 1976).

13. *See* M. Francis Mannion, "Penance And Reconciliation: A Systemic Analysis," *Worship* 60 (1986) 98-119.

14. *Ibid.* 104-5.

15. *See Didache,* c. 115.

16. *See* Laurence Brett, *Redeemed Creation* (Wilmington, Del.: Michael Glazier: 1984); John R. Gilbert, "The Reconciliation Service: A Reflection on Pastoral Experience as a Theological Source," *Worship* 59 (1985) 59-65.

CHAPTER EIGHT

Moments of Healing

Just a quick look at our cultural milieu will confirm that we are indeed a death-denying people. We drink and drug ourselves out of awareness, camouflage all tell-tale signs of aging, continue to pollute our lungs and bodies with toxins in bold defiance of medical advances, and wile away precious hours shopping, complaining, and developing intimate relationships with fictitious people who live in our TV sets. Ernest Becker's 1974 Pulitzer Prize winning book *The Denial of Death* examined the tremendous philosophical, psychological, and societal impact of this denial. Against this backdrop of cultural denial, we expect that the Christian's attitude toward sickness and death, rooted in the foundational principle of the death and resurrection of the Lord, would stand in stark contrast.

Attitudes toward Sickness and Death

Anthropologists, sociologists, and psychologists, as well as theologians, are in agreement that death is the singularly most profound experience a human being can encounter. Death drives us to the limits of our existence and plunges us into the depths of mystery. Each time we enter into the experience of death and dying, accompanying family, friends, or celebrities on that final journey, we come face to face with our own mortality, and on some level rehearse our own death. Our rituals surrounding sickness and death testify to this as well. Death and burial rituals, known since paleolithic times, are so critical to the experience of death in the human community, that anthropologist Margaret Mead knows of no people without a ritual with which to deal with death. In some cultures birth is treated casually, but death is always critical.[1]

In order to understand the significance of death in the human community in general, as opposed to a particular religious group, anthropologists turn their attention to the indigenous peoples of undeveloped (as opposed to developing) areas of the world. These pagans, like those whose artifacts date back to antiquity, generally view death with fear, not hope, and look upon the corpse with aversion rather than affection.

Elisabeth Kübler-Ross, in her classic work *On Death and Dying*, explains this phenomenon in psychological terms. Since the human unconscious cannot fathom the possibility of its own death, it attributes the ending of life to some malicious intervention. In itself, death has been connected with evil—sometimes even personifying evil—and calls out for retribution and punishment.[2]

In that brief anthropological synthesis we can find basic plots for any number of novels or plays, along with the root of superstitions that even plague the Christian community. The ministry of the Church in the face of sickness and death has been tremendously hampered by superstition. For many people calling for the priest was perceived to be synonymous with calling down the Angel of Death. At the very moment when people were most in need of the Church's ministry, their fear of death kept at a distance the sacramental encounter with Jesus as well.

We see the same dis-ease with disease in the medical profession as well. It is a physician's personal discomfort with his or her own mortality that keeps patients at a distance. They will speak about the liver cancer in Room 394, relating to diseased tissue rather than suffering people. These fears multiply, lead us in dizzying circles, and condemn too many members of our community to endless days in needless isolation. When an elderly gentleman in our parish was hospitalized I went to visit him. "I'm never going to leave this hospital," he told me, "I know I'm going to die."

"How do you know that?" I asked. "Did the doctors tell you so?"

"They don't have to," Dan replied. "The doctors and nurses never come in to see me anymore. I know they've given up on me."

Although both his observation and conclusion were accurate, I don't think his reasoning was. I doubt that anyone had given up on him. Fear keeps people away—fear of entertaining death, of coming too close to such blatant reality.

For a number of years I worked as a volunteer in a local hospice. There I came to know a wonderful community of people who were willing companions on life's final journey. Along that way I also came to know our patients' families and friends, many of whom were too paralyzed by their own fear of death to be able to embrace the suffering person. Walter's story is most memorable to me.

It was his sixty-fifth birthday and his family held a big party in the lounge, inviting many of Walter's friends and co-workers. The original site of Walter's cancer, as he told me, was the prostate, but by the time of the party it had advanced very far. Walter was paralyzed from the waist down, he tired very quickly, and since the cancer had even invaded his liver, his complexion was beginning to yellow considerably. After spending some time at the party, Walter asked to be returned to his room, and I sat with him there, while the party continued at the other end of the wing. A friend who had been late for the festivities stopped in for a visit. "You look terrific, Walter! I haven't seen you looking so well for months. You look as though you're ready to get up from that bed and walk out of here." The friend went on at a great rate, totally oblivious to Walter's worsening physical condition as well as to the tears that gently began to roll down Walter's face.

When his friend finally left, Walter poured out to me all the distress he felt at such inconsiderate visits. He was furious and thought that his friend's visit was completely self-serving and totally lacking in compassion. "He didn't come to see me," Walter added, "he came to see what he wants to be—a miraculous survivor." This incident, of course, was only a catalyst enabling Walter to surface all the feelings that had been building up inside him over the course of his illness.

I've heard countless patients scream out at their families "I'm dying!" hoping to break through that shield of denial. It just compounds the tragedy of dying to become involved in these intense emotional disputes which have at their root each person's fear of death. Fear leads to denial and that erects walls where there should be bridges, and leads to coldness where there should be tenderness.

The pariah that cancer once was now walks our streets clothed as AIDS. As Susan Sontag has observed, "AIDS has banalized cancer."[3] Our society seems to be treating AIDS patients more as criminals than victims of disease. Once again we see that fear has displaced compassion along with spirituality.

Shaping a Spirituality

We look to the person of Jesus, whose life gives shape to our spirituality, to see how he responded to sickness and death. We recall his encounters with the blind man, lepers, the woman who had been hemorrhaging for years, children near death, and his friend Lazarus. We also remember the deep fears held by the people of Jesus' time. They saw sickness or physical deformity as signs of evil, and literally banished the sick and suffering in order not to contaminate themselves with evil and visit sickness upon themselves as well. Jesus TOUCHED these people! He also cured, but to the people of his day the fact that he touched them was even more remarkable than his curing them.

The readings for the Third Sunday of Lent (Cycle A), which include the story of the raising of Lazarus, focus on death, and are used in celebrating the third scrutiny of the RCIA. With outstretched hands we pray over the elect.

> Lord Jesus,
> by raising Lazarus from the dead
> you showed that you came that we might have life
> and have it more abundantly.
>
> Free from the grasp of death
> those who await your life-giving sacraments
> and deliver them from the spirit of corruption.[4]

The Christian approach to death, while being attentive to the basic human fear associated with physical mortality, must underscore our fundamental belief in spiritual immortality. Death, we claim to believe repeatedly in the liturgy, is not an end; it marks the beginning of the life for which we have all been yearning.

Using Elisabeth Kübler-Ross's interpretation that death, even the death of a close relative or friend, takes us to the limit of our human existence, we must add the Christian correlative. When we are taken to our limits, there is God!

When my brother-in-law died last year, the victim of a cancer that destroyed his robust body in less than a month, I was given a great gift. Bob had been raised a Baptist, and although he had long ago given up active participation in any church communion, he respected our beliefs and my work. I consider the gift his final affirmation of my commitment to God and the Church. No voices spoke to me and no visions appeared before me, but I was overwhelmed by a confident assurance, so strong that I can relate it to nothing else, that no one dies alone. At the moment of death, God comes to us, embraces us, and leads us home.

That gift coupled with my faith in the Gospel shapes not only my spirituality, but along with it the way I minister to others: my students, the dying, the grieving, all the people I encounter on this life journey. The same is true for the rest of the Christian community. Just as our personal experience and expression of faith gives shape to the catechumenate and the process of incorporating new members into the community of believers, so it will likewise characterize our ministry to our sick and dying members as well.

Spirituality and Ministry

When a family member or a person in the hospital is near death or takes a sudden turn for the worse, our immediate reaction is usually "Call Father!" At the moment in our larger cities and most suburban areas that is still a possibility, but in vast areas of the United States there are simply not enough Fathers to make that a reasonable assumption.

Present legislation still determines that the priest is the only possible minister of the sacramental anointing of the sick, but what the members of our community will have experienced through the catechumenal process is that while the priest is the principal minister of the community, he is not its only minister. Ministry to the sick and dying is the responsibility of the entire community, and is carried out on many different levels.

When the elderly gentleman to whom she had brought the Eucharist for several years lay close to death, the family called Margaret. They knew she had been there each Sunday to pray with their father and to talk about the exciting life that would soon begin for him. She had eased his fears about the passage through death to new life, and they thought she was the person to call as the time of his death neared. We will probably be hearing more stories like that in the years to come, not because there will be fewer priests, but because the ministry begun by Jesus will be continued by all those who follow in his way. Jesus taught us that we can all be ministers of consolation. As it has been recently noted, "aside from remote petitions at worship or a passing word of condolence, members of the local faith community are seldom invited into the dying or grieving process."[5] That is neither the attitude Jesus fostered nor the one fostered by our experience with the RCIA. Appropriate ministry by the local faith community to the sick and dying requires no great gifts or advanced degrees beyond a willingness to be present to others.

Will a time come when we have extraordinary ministers of anointing?[6] Surely that is a possibility, and theologians and canonists have already begun to discuss and research the possibility. We will have to be content, however, with living on into the final answer to that question.

Anointing of the Sick

The Rite of Anointing and Pastoral Care of the Sick was approved by Paul VI in November of 1972 in the Apostolic Constitution *Sacram*

Unctionem infirmorum, which placed the rite into an appropriate historical and pastoral context. The rite was published by the Congregation for
Divine Worship in December of that year.[7]

Citing the allusion in Mark 6:13 as evidence of Jesus' institution of
this sacrament, the preaching of the Apostle James is traditionally cited
as the earliest evidence of this sacrament's existence.

> Is there anyone sick among you? Let him call for the elders of the Church,
> and let them pray over him and anoint him in the name of the Lord. This
> prayer, made in faith, will save the sick man. The Lord will restore his health,
> and if he has committed any sins, they will be forgiven (Jas 5:14-15).

Pastoral Aspect

An important dimension of our approach to the anointing of the sick is
an awareness that sickness itself can be sacramental. David Power has
expressed it well:

> In the sacrament of the sick what is at stake is the sacramentality of sick-
> ness itself, or, perhaps it would be better to say, the mystery which is re-
> vealed in the sick person who lives through this experience. In other words,
> the accent is not on healing, nor on forgiving, nor on preparing for death.
> It is on the sick person, who through this experience discovers God in a
> particular way and reveals this to the community.[8]

The author goes on to emphasize that the "sacramental meaning inherent
in Christian liturgy is not something added on to nature, it is drawn out
of it."[9] We can surely see that this statement is applicable to our discussion of the other sacraments here, as well as to the revised Order of Christian Funerals.

Order of Christian Funerals

Following the recommendations made by the Second Vatican Council in
its Constitution on the Sacred Liturgy, along with all of the sacraments,
changes were made in the funeral liturgy as well. The decree enacting this
reform, The *Ordo Exsequiarium* (August 15, 1969) emphasized the point
that the Church's funeral rites should "not only commend the dead to God,
but also support the Christian hope of the people and give witness to its
faith in the future resurrection of the baptized with Christ."[10]

The Order of Christian Funerals is a complete revision of the English
translation of the *Ordo Exsequiarium.* Rather than being a new rite, this
edition actually brings a sense of order to the rites as they were previously

revised. The rites are rearranged and developed so that they represent a cohesive theology of death and Christian burial, and can be of greater use to the Christian community.

The Order of Christian Funerals underscores the fact that all members of the Church share in the ministry of consolation: caring for the dying, praying for the dead, and comforting those who mourn.[11] Although this ministry primarily involves active participation in the funeral rites (vigil, funeral liturgy, committal), the order suggests other possibilities for members of the community, such as prayers at time of death, a ritual for gathering in the presence of the body, in addition to morning prayer and evening prayer from the Office of the Dead. The Order provides us with a spiritual and theological framework for celebrating the death of a Christian, while the liturgies within the Order give a structure to the Church's ministry of bereavement. As the Order begins to be implemented in the coming months, we will see how these expanded rituals intersect with the dimension of communal involvement developed in our experience of the rituals of the RCIA. This will expand the expression of ourselves as a caring community.

NOTES

1. Margaret Mead, "Ritual and Social Crisis," in *Roots of Ritual*, ed. James Shaughnessy (Grand Rapids: Eerdmans, 1973) 89–90.

2. Elizabeth Kubler-Ross, *On Death and Dying* (New York: Macmillan, 1969) 2.

3. Susan Sontag, *AIDS and its Metaphors* (New York: Farrar, Straus and Giroux, 1989) 44.

4. RCIA, no. 175.

5. Herbert Anderson and Edward Foley, "Liturgy and Pastoral Care: The Parable of Dying and Grieving" *New Theology Review* 1/4 (November 1988) 18.

6. The Apostolic Tradition of Hippolytus (c. 215) appears to give some evidence that individuals other than bishops and presbyters anointed. See John J. Ziegler, "Who Can Anoint the Sick" *Worship* 61 (January 1987) 25–44.

7. For an excellent study of the tradition, reforms, and present understanding of this sacrament see Charles W. Gusmer, *And You Visited Me: Sacramental Ministry to the Sick and the Dying* (New York: Pueblo, 1984, 1990).

8. David Power, "Let the Sick Man Call," *Heythrop Journal* 19 (1978) 262.

9. *Ibid.*

10. Congregation for Divine Worship, Decree, August 15, 1969.

11. *Order of Christian Funerals* [OCF] (Washington: International Commission on English in the Liturgy, 1985, 1989) no. 8.

CHAPTER NINE

Sacraments of Vocation in a New Age

For centuries in the Roman Catholic tradition, the word baptism has been virtually synonymous with infant baptism, conjuring up for us the picture of an unhappy, even frightened, squirming infant. Some people mistakenly draw the conclusion that all the RCIA changes is the person being baptized, that we simply change the person in our picture from an infant to an adult. The previous chapters here have attempted to demonstrate that such is far from the case. With the RCIA in place not only must the entire picture be changed, but along with it the vocabulary used to describe that picture. For example, increasingly our pictures would have the church filled with people celebrating the Great Vigil of Easter. Having witnessed the weekly dismissal of those preparing for membership, the community would be excited at the prospect of welcoming the elect into full membership and having them join in the Liturgy of the Eucharist for the first time.

Instead of focusing only on the individual, as we did in another era when we saw baptism in isolation, our lens must now be adjusted to focus on the ecclesial community into which the individual is being incorporated, for that is where all of the sacraments make fullest theological sense. The Church is the on-going reality of God dwelling among us in time, and thus the Church is a sacrament in the very truest sense of the word. It is in the Church as sacrament that "we live and move and have our being." Therefore, since the Church occupies this position of primary importance, that is where our attention should be focused.[1]

Once our focus has shifted, it becomes more strikingly obvious, for a series of inter-related reasons, that the community itself needs to take responsibility for incorporating new members.

105

First of all, it is logical for us to conclude that the strength and effectiveness of the entire community hinges on those who are incorporated into the community. It naturally follows that the entire community should be actively involved in and concerned about its continued existence, which is to a large extent determined by those being incorporated into the community. Furthermore, only the members of the community really know the demands membership places on them, and thus they are the best witnesses to those interested in becoming members.

Though in differing degrees, every member shares in this ministry. Catechists, selected by the community, direct the course of the catechumenate, but all members are called to witness their faith in everyday life, and it is this ministry that is a powerful force in enabling catechumens and neophytes to see themselves as functioning members of the community. Through participating in this process of conversion, we have seen that other members of the community are renewed, recognizing that they are continually being called to conversion themselves.

As any member of the Christian community should easily recognize, however, converting to Christianity does not mean entering into a static state of being Christian, but rather into a dynamic process of constantly becoming Christian. We know that this holds true for infants as well as adults. Tertullian was not only speaking of his own generation when he said that "Christians are made, not born."[2] For this reason our vocabulary must reflect the dynamic nature of the Christian vocation, and as Christians we must begin to think in the category of initiatory process rather than limiting our attention to the single rite of baptism.

We have seen that with the RCIA the normative process of initiation is established, for it is in the presence of the Christian community that the process of incorporating an adult into the community is celebrated most ideally. The process, truly a function of the entire community, recognizes the gradual nature of human adaptability, and responds to a mature commitment to the Christian life. Individuals become members of the grace-filled community as soon as they are enrolled in the catechumenate. Not only are catechumens entitled to a Christian burial, but should two catechumens decide to marry, or a catechumen decide to marry someone outside the community, the official rite of marriage is used.[3] As catechumens they enter into the process of becoming Christians—a process that will only end when they enter the heavenly kingdom.[4] Once they have learned the ways of the community and consider themselves prepared to live as full members, their faith-commitment is celebrated in the three sacraments of the initiation ritual: baptism, confirmation, and Eucharist.

In this developmental model other sacraments and aspects of ecclesial life take on new dimensions as well, emphasizing the fact that the Church continually evokes the Lord's presence in herself, in her sacraments, and in her people. This model has particular application in the area of special vocations that necessitate a radical change in lifestyle. It has been noted that when the catechumenate seemed to disappear from the Church, it actually migrated to religious communities.[5] In theory, a formation process that somewhat resembled the RCIA was operative in religious houses. Religious formation, however, was still person-centered rather than community-centered. The developmental model found in the RCIA is more holistic. Using such a model, formation within a particular religious community takes on a deeper dimension for the individual, the community, and the Church. The same holds true for marriage, where the model has yet to be applied in actual practice, and for initiation into the community of ordained presbyters. Each of these can be viewed as analogous to initiation into the Christian community.

Initiation into a Religious Community

There are various ways in which one can see the parallels between the RCIA and religious formation.[6] As noted in *Perfectae Caritatis*, public commitment to a consecrated life in a religious community builds on the baptismal commitment:

> The members of each community should recall above everything else that by their profession of the evangelical counsels they have given answer to a divine call to live for God alone not only by dying to sin . . . but also by renouncing the world. They have handed over their entire lives to God's service in an act of special consecration which is deeply rooted in their baptismal consecration and which provides an ampler manifestation of it.[7]

Who was aware of this great celebration known as religious profession in the past? Who witnessed these rituals of profound dedication? To ecclesial communities religious life was a complete mystery. *The Nun's Story*, a best-seller which was filmed, and played in movie theaters across the country in the late 1950s, was the closest many people—Catholics included—came to knowing what went on behind the convent walls. Audrey Hepburn portrayed Sister Luke, and we followed her journey from entrance into the community, through the stages of formation, to religious profession, and out to the mission. Apart from the viewing audience of that film, only members of a sister's immediate family had any inkling of the dramatic rituals that formed the core of religious life.

Although today the names of these stages often vary among religious congregations, the stages of religious formation show a structural similarity to the stages of the RCIA, as outlined below.[8]

PARALLELS IN RELIGIOUS FORMATION

RCIA	RELIGIOUS COMMUNITY
pre-catechumenate	affiliate program
catechumenate	associate membership (postulancy)
enlightenment	canonical novitiate
mystagogy	first vows

To stop there, however, is to eclipse the full importance of the analogue.

As a slow maturation process governs biological life, it likewise governs spiritual life, and even if an individual was baptized as an infant, the process of coming to a mature faith is still necessary. This is true of all Christian life, but more so for those called to live out their Christian life in a more radical way. Members of religious communities are also formed by a slow process of maturation. Given the proper environment and nourishment, growth from within will be fostered.

As has been shown previously with specific reference to the RCIA,[9] each stage of the process has its own reality and allows the individual to develop in a particular dimension. Furthermore, each stage of the process should also be punctuated by a public ritual, ideally within the celebration of the Eucharist.

a. The *first stage* consists of coming to know the community in its widest scope through its founders, its members, its charism, and its spirit. One attempts to discern whether or not one is called to embody those same characteristics in living out the Gospel message.

b. Believing that he or she is called to become part of the community, the individual asks to be received as a candidate in the same way one asks to be received as a catechumen, for the source of the call is the same:

> You have followed God's light and the way of the Gospel now lies open before you. Set your feet firmly on that path and acknowledge the living God, who truly speaks to everyone. Walk in the light of Christ and learn to trust in his wisdom. Commit your lives daily to his care, so that you may come to believe in him with all your heart.
>
> This is the way of faith along which Christ will lead you in love toward eternal life. Are you prepared to begin this journey today under the guidance of Christ?[10]

Although the words are proper to the RCIA, their intent is applicable to the parallel structure, and the *second stage*, therefore, brings one into the community structure *per se*, where one can learn more intimately and more fully the way of life proper to the community, often by engaging, to a limited extent, in its prayer and ministry.

c. Having been "strengthened by God's grace and supported by the community's example and prayers,"[11] the candidate asks to move to a deeper level of preparation:

> God is always faithful to those he calls: now it is your duty, as it is ours, both to be faithful to him in return and to strive courageously to reach the fullness of ..th, which your election opens up before you.[12]

Th , . *third stage* of the formation process is more dedicated to allowing t. ..dividual to develop spiritually than any of the other stages. Since one has become more comfortable with the life and work of the community, one is allowed more time to prepare oneself for public consecration.

d. The process does not end after one has made a public commitment, uniting oneself to the community. Rather, in the *fourth stage* one reflects more deeply on the commitment made as one begins to live as a full member of the community. This stage, therefore, really begins the process of on-going formation which continues throughout one's life in the community.

Just as the RCIA benefited the local church and the universal Church as well, so does the religious formation process. Members of religious communities are continually called to renewal as they become involved in the formation of newer members of the community. This is one way of fulfilling the intention of the bishops at Vatican II:

> Throughout their lives religious should labor earnestly to perfect their spiritual, doctrinal, and professional development. As far as possible, superiors should provide them with the opportunity, the resources, and the time to do so.[13]

In order to help individuals become incorporated into the community, members who are involved in the process must re-define for themselves the community's charism and its mission or life-style. Consequently, they will deepen their own understanding and experience of those dimensions of community life. To limit this opportunity to only a small team is to deny the larger community a significant opportunity for continuing spiritual growth. As the role of the formation team could parallel the role of the catechists in the catechumenate, other aspects of the RCIA model are also available for application. The role of sponsorship, for example, is one that could be highlighted and expanded as it is in the RCIA,[14] to the benefit of both the candidate and the community.

Initiation into the Married Community

Although no concrete liturgical structures or stages for marriage have yet been delineated by ecclesiastical authorities, the RCIA model could be adapted for use with engaged couples even in a local parish community. Sociologically, cultural patterning in the United States provides four distinct stages leading to marriage, so that we could apply the RCIA model simply by placing them in a liturgical and ecclesial context. With the divorce rate hovering about the fifty percent mark in the United States today, even among Catholics, it is time for us to give some serious attention to our approach to the sacrament of marriage. Marriage among Christians ought to be much more than a social convention, but that is often how it is regarded among those of marriageable age.

For almost ten years now I have been teaching undergraduate courses in both liturgy and marriage. Class size is regularly fifty or sixty students, although one semester I had 134 students in the marriage course. As I move into the section of the course that deals specifically with the liturgical celebration of the sacrament, I ask how many of the students consider themselves to be active members of the believing community. Generally about ten percent would label themselves as such. The remainder participate in community worship on special holidays (Easter and Christmas) and whenever else they feel so inclined. They find church worship boring, participants hypocrites, and themselves too busy with work or in need of sleep. I next ask how many, if they marry, will ask to receive the sacrament of marriage. As you might expect, the responses are quite different. Only the rare student would prefer civil to sacramental marriage. "Why?" I ask, appearing to be baffled by their response.

"Our church is so pretty, and I've dreamed my whole life of walking down that aisle."

"I want to wear a beautiful white wedding gown and have six bridesmaids dressed in different pastel colors. That doesn't fit at City Hall."

"It would kill my parents if I didn't get married in the Church."

"It's traditional!"

Those are the usual responses I receive. Only once have I received a faith-filled response. It came on a warm Friday in April, shortly after Easter break. I posed that usual question to a student sitting in the first row. Unfortunately, only I could see her face. It was a study in thoughtful deliberation. While she considered my question, her look changed from concern to amazement. "I guess I really believe!" she exclaimed, surprising even herself with the response. The class was stunned, and that gave me the opportunity to probe a little deeper into the dimensions of faith she was beginning to sense.

The Rite of Marriage itself provides the imperative for asking such probing questions as well as for implementing a developmental model for approaching sacramental marriage:

> Priests should first of all strengthen and nourish the faith of those about to be married, for the sacrament of Matrimony presupposes and demands faith.[15]

The spiritual dimension of marriage, as an extension of Christian life in general, can be approached as a further deepening of one's faith commitment made in Baptism. The experience provided by the catechumenate has demonstrated for us how this takes place, and therefore the model could serve as a matrix for enabling the faith of those about to be married to be deepened likewise.

The cultural stages leading to marriage mentioned earlier are:

- courtship
- engagement
- sacramental celebration
- honeymoon/mystagogy

One can quickly see how they tend to parallel the stages of the RCIA.

Since the members of the married community live out their Christian commitment in a unique way, they are most suited to help in preparing other members of the community for married life. This was even noted by the bishops of Vatican II:

> the apostolate of married persons and of families is of unique importance for the Church and civil society. Among the multiple activities of the family apostolate may be . . . help to engaged couples in preparing themselves better for marriage.[16]

In home pre-Cana, as some parishes refer to their process, has gone a long way to bring a communal dimension to preparation for marriage. What yet remains necessary to be done, however, is to make both marriage preparation and enrichment a corporate responsibility.

Imagine the possibilities. Young couples seriously considering marriage could meet together periodically. Helping them in answering their questions and aiding their discernment would be members of the pre-Cana team, composed of married couples, spiritual directors, counselors, and medical personnel, for example. The members of the larger parish community would regularly be asked to pray for all those discerning their call to the married state.

When a couple has decided to become engaged, even though they might celebrate their decision romantically in a charming French restaurant, they would bring their decision to the believing community. One way in which I envision this happening would begin when the newly engaged couple visits the parish priest to make arrangements for the marriage ritual. Soon afterwards, at a Sunday Eucharist, following the homily, the couple would be introduced to the community, and their engagement blessed[17] in the presence of the community. In the General Intercessions the community would be asked to pray for them and for all couples preparing for marriage, which would bring the needs of engaged couples before the community.

Depending on the number of people involved, perhaps all of the couples to be married in a particular month would begin meeting together, along with one or two married couples, with the intention of sharing faith rather than information. Music directors might already be having such meetings to plan the practical details of the wedding, but there is much more sacramental preparation we could be doing quite easily.

Once again, as members of the married community help others in the process of becoming ready to make a public commitment to live a consecrated life, their own understanding of and commitment to married life will be renewed and strengthened.

Sacraments as Ecclesial Events

As a Church community we run into some rough roads when we begin to delineate between public and private events. Theologically, sacraments are never private events, for they have their locus in the believing community. Culturally, however, we tend to regard weddings (and often funerals) as private events to which one must be formally invited. A private sacrament is an anomaly, and as a community we must begin to address this cultural/theological conflict more firmly.

When I first begin to discuss this anomaly with students in my marriage course, they immediately become indignant. Their whole lives they have been dreaming of their wedding day, and their dreams have not included all the neighbors showing up in dirty jeans and sweatshirts. Once I assure them that people attending a wedding would be intelligent enough to dress appropriately, I ask them to begin brainstorming ways in which we might begin to make the sacrament of marriage more of an ecclesial event. Their ideas never cease to amaze me. Let me share some of them with you, hoping that they will stimulate your thinking with regard to what might be feasible in your pastoral situation.

Their first and most obvious suggestion is to inform the community of the nuptial Mass and invite them to attend. While the bans of marriage are traditionally published in the parish bulletin or listed in some other prominent place, rarely is the date or time of the wedding posted. Where notice is given, one generally finds it listed in the parish bulletin the previous week, which hardly seems to be inviting attendance. In addition to encouraging attendance, my students often suggest that the community's participation be invited as well. By that they mean that members of the community would serve as Eucharistic ministers or in the music ministry.

Another focus of my students' attention is the General Intercessions. Here they see two inter-related possibilities. The General Intercessions prayed at the nuptial Mass, they suggest, should express in some way the relationship between the couple being married and the church building or the parish community. Our sacraments are not celebrated in catering halls, but sometimes they seem to be so distanced from the sacredness of the space or the presence of the community of believers that they might as well be taking place there. Often the bride was raised in the parish community, or one (or both) of them has been living and worshipping in the community for a time. Some simple attention could be given to this relationship in the General Intercessions.

More importantly, however, they consider the General Intercessions prayed in the larger community on Sunday. Rarely is any mention ever given in prayer of the couples married during the previous week. Young couples need the prayers of the Church, and encouraging such prayer in the community would help to emphasize not only the sacramental character of marriage, but also the community's role in the support of members of the married community.

An interesting suggestion was made in one class about the collection. Again, they saw two dimensions to this. The students suggested that a collection be taken up at the nuptial Mass, either as a contribution to the parish or for the needs of the poor in the area. Their reason for suggesting this was to emphasize the dictates of the gospel as well as to underscore once again the relationship to the parish community.

Their other suggestion was to take up a collection at the parish Mass the following Sunday and give the proceeds to the couples married that week as the parish's gift to the newlyweds. I don't think that the suggestion was born of greed, but of an attempt to involve the parish community more in the celebration of the sanctity of marriage. The best way they could see to express that was with a gift.

Another suggestion they made concerned the presence and participation of children. They observed that children, with the exception of the flower girl and ring bearer, are rarely involved even in attending weddings. While wedding receptions are traditionally adult affairs, the students regretted that the nuptial Mass is often treated similarly. Not only did they think that children should be present, but they thought that the children, as symbols of the fruit of marriage, should have a place of prominence, not hidden in the back far from view.

Once the students grasped the concept of marriage in the midst of the community, supported by the community in faith, hope, and charity, their ideas came flooding out. Would such an awareness encourage couples to work more at their marriage, and begin to lower the divorce rate? That is another of those questions for which we must live on into the answer.

Initiation into the Presbyteral Community

The sacrament most hidden from the ecclesial community is probably the sacrament of holy orders. Few people have ever attended an ordination, and fewer still seem to know when ordinations are being celebrated or who is preparing for ordination. This situation is worlds removed from the concept of leadership in the first centuries of Christianity.

From the earliest days of the Church the ministry of leadership was directly related and responsive to the needs of the community. The first instance of this is recorded in the Acts of the Apostles when it appears that the needs of one segment of the community were being neglected in the daily distribution of food. The problem was brought before the assembled community, and after praying for guidance, they reached the decision to appoint deacons who would attend to the physical needs of the community, freeing the apostles and disciples involved in preaching to attend to the spiritual needs of the community.

As the Church grew, so did its needs for leadership.[18] When leadership, recognized as one of the differing gifts of the Holy Spirit, was seen in an individual member of the community, the community asked to have that person ordained, and consequently he would preside at their celebrations of Eucharist. The emphasis was on community leadership not limited to celebrating the Eucharist.

Vocation Crisis?

We have been reading a great deal in recent years about a vocation crisis. Generally I consider the crisis to be illusory. It does not seem reasonable to me that God has ceased to call people to service. When I see the large numbers of people responding to ministry in the Church as lectors, Eucharist ministers, catechists, musicians, and ministers of hospitality, and when I see people coming early to morning Mass carrying their office books, joining privately in the universal morning prayer of the Church, I fail to see any crisis in vocations. Of course there are fewer men willing to serve as ordained presbyters in the Church, but it seems to me that that has less to do with God's call than with our response.

Last year I gave a presentation on the ministry of the laity at a local parish where I am well known. At the conclusion of the presentation, after many questions had already been asked, a woman raised her hand to be recognized. She took great offense at the concept of lay ministry which she saw as dishonoring the priesthood. She was adamant in her position that my presentation was an attempt to squeeze out the priests. "Do you pray for vocations?" she finally bellowed.

Calmly I responded, "Prayer is not enough. Vocations need to be fostered, and that is very difficult in our consumer-oriented society." I went on to ask how many people urged their sons at least to consider priesthood. In response to that question I could see many people in the audience pale.

"You want your sons to be economically successful, so you urge them to be doctors, lawyers, or accountants. Above all, you want to be grandparents. This doesn't foster vocations to the priesthood!"

We have an attitude crisis, not a vocation crisis, and if we, as a community, were to improve our attitude toward the ordained ministry, we would be better able to foster the vocations God has already granted us.

Role of the Community

In the United States today we have two types of seminary structures: freestanding seminaries, and university-centered seminaries. Although freestanding seminaries are more common, and encouraged by the Holy See, they tend to create an impediment to developing a relationship with a local community that is an essential preparation for ministry in the Church.

A means of fostering appropriate preparation, and at the same time developing the role of the community in relation to this sacrament, would be a process of field placement. During each of the candidate's four years at the seminary it seems advisable that the candidate be missioned to a different parish. Although they would continue to live at the seminary, they would develop a limited relationship with the parish community— have dinner at the rectory one night a week, attend the principal Eucharist on Sunday, learn about the various functions and organizations of the parish, and so on. Not only would this give seminary graduates four different experiences of the life and expectations of parish ministry, but it would give the parishioners a means of supporting those preparing for ordination. Even where students from various dioceses study at regional seminaries it is possible to provide this component to seminary education. Perhaps a combination of field placement in a parish close to the seminary with adoption by a parish in the home diocese would be realistic for that situation.

Many fine young men are preparing for the priesthood in our seminaries. They study hard and struggle against the lure of the culture which hardly seems to support the values of poverty or celibacy. Communities need to know these young men and support them in prayer. Their willingness to stand as a sign of contradiction to our society by becoming members of the presbyteral community may serve as an example for others who might be open to considering a response to God's call themselves. We need to celebrate those who are responding to this call with much more strength than we mourn those who are not. Affirmation by the communities whom they will one day serve is an important ingredient in this process of incorporation.

NOTES

1. Raymond Kemp, "The Rite of Christian Initiation of Adults at Ten Years," *Worship* 56 (1982) 309–27.

2. Tertullian, *De Baptismo* [*DB*] no. 18.5, trans. and ed. Ernest Evans (London: SPCK, 1964) 39.

3. RCIA, no. 47.

4. In the case of infant baptism, the Catholic school or the CCD program becomes a metaphorical catechumenate.

5. Aidan Kavanagh, "Christian Initiation in Post-Conciliar Roman Catholicism: A Brief Report," *Studia Liturgica* 12 (1977) 109.

6. *See* C. Bouchard, "Journey of Faith: Initial Religious Formation as an Extension of the New Rite of Initiation of Adults," *Review for Religious* 36 (1977) 592–99; Thomas J. Talley, "Ordination in Today's Thinking," *Studia Liturgica* 13 (1979) 4–10.

7. *Perfectae Caritatis* [*PC*] no. 5, 470.

8. Although the names given to the stages might vary from community to community, the type of relationship they describe is constant.

9. *See* pp. 36–37 in this book.

10. RCIA, no. 52.

11. RCIA, no. 130.

12. RCIA, no. 133.

13. *PC*, no. 18, 479.

14. See Dujarier, "Sponsorship," in *Adult Baptism and the Catechumenate*, Concilium, vol. 22, ed. Johannes Wagner (New York: Paulist Press, 1967).

15. *Rite of Marriage* [*RM*] (Washington: United States Catholic Conference, 1974).

16. *AA*, no. 11, 502–3.

17. *See Book of Blessings* (Washington: United States Catholic Conference, 1988) 236.

18. For an excellent study of the history of the Sacrament of Holy Orders see Nathan Mitchell, *Mission and Ministry: History and Theology in the Sacrament of Order* (Wilmington, Michael Glazier, 1986).

In Conclusion

The Fathers of Vatican II led us to the threshold of a new era in ecclesial history, and challenged the community to recognize and respond to the dynamism that characterizes the Church in its essence. It is precisely that quality of ecclesial life that is addressed in the Rite of Christian Initiation of Adults. That relationship is in keeping with the tradition of the Church, which has continually manifested its essence in and through its process of incorporating new members.

As a dynamic community of believers, the Church has reacted and developed according to the needs and demands of the changing historical situation, whether the response has been one of advancement or one of retrenchment. This era in ecclesial history is no different. The needs of the present day that call for continued spiritual growth, fuller participation of the laity in ecclesial ministry, and a serious approach to faith-commitment, find an appropriate response in the RCIA.

Not only does the RCIA respond to the needs of today, but it also prepares and challenges the community to move confidently into tomorrow. It does this by establishing a model upon which answers to questions concerning other areas of ecclesial life can be formulated. This appropriation is possible because the rite acknowledges the principle that all life is in process, and therefore the members of the community are continually being formed as Christians in their own spiritual journey and through helping others on the journey. That dynamic growth principle, integral to the human condition, finds its expression in post-Vatican II liturgical life.

Above all else, the RCIA teaches the community to reverence each person's journey of faith. Some candidates may travel by a long and winding road. They may appear to veer off course at times, or get lost along the way. Some journeys may take more time than others before the sacraments of initiation are ready to be celebrated. God is the travel agent, and as we have been shown many times over, God's ways are not our ways.

Bibliography

Primary Sources

A. **Roman Ritual:**

Order of Christian Funerals. Washington: International Commission on English in the Liturgy, 1989.
Rite of Baptism for Children. Washington: United States Catholic Conference, 1969.
Rite of Christian Initiation of Adults. Washington: United States Catholic Conference, 1986.
Rite of Confirmation. Washington: United States Catholic Conference, 1971.
Rite of Marriage. Washington: United States Catholic Conference, 1970.

B. **Ecclesial Documents:**

Code of Canon Law. Washington: Canon Law Society of America, 1983.
Documents on the Liturgy 1963–1979. Collegeville: Liturgical Press, 1982.
The Documents of Vatican II. Edited by Walter M. Abbott. New York: America Press, 1966.

C. **Papal Documentation:**

Paul VI. "Closing Address," *The Living Light* 15 (1978) 98–100.
_____. *Divinae Consortium Naturae. L'Osservatore Romano* (Eng) 38 (September 23, 1971) 4–5.
_____. *Evangelii Nutiandi.* Washington: United States Catholic Conference, 1976.
John Paul II. *Catechesi Tradendae. Origins* 9 (1979) 329–48.
_____. *Christifideles Laici. Origins* 18 (1989) 561–95.

D. **Patristic Texts:**

Augustine, *City of God.* Trans. Gerald G. Walsh, Demetrius B. Zema, Grace Monahan, and Daniel J. Honan. Garden City: Doubleday, 1958.

_____. *Tractates on the Gospel According to St. John*, 2 volumes. Trans. John Gibb. Edinburgh: T. and T. Clark, 1873.

Chrysostom, St. John. *Baptismal Instructions*. Trans. and ed. P. W. Harkins. Vol. 3: Ancient Christian Writers. New York: Newman Press, 1963.

Cyprian, *Letters*. Trans. Rose Bernard Donna. Vol. 51: Fathers of the Church. Washington: Catholic University of America Press, 1964.

_____. *De Lapsis and De Ecclesiae Catholicae Unitate*. Trans. and ed. Maurice Bevenot. Oxford: Clarendon, 1971.

Hippolytus. *The Apostolic Tradition of St. Hippolytus*. Ed. Gregory Dix. London: SPCK, 1968.

Tertullian. *Apologetical Works*. Trans. Rudolph Arbesmann, et al. Volume 10: Fathers of the Church. New York: Fathers of the Church, 1950.

_____. *Disciplinary, Moral, and Ascetical Works*. Trans. Rudolph Arbesmann, et al. Volume 40: Fathers of the Church. New York: Fathers of the Church, 1959.

_____. *Fathers of the Third Century*. Ed. Alexander Roberts and James Donaldson. Vol. 4: Ante-Nicene Fathers. New York: Charles Scribner's Sons, 1925.

_____. *Homily on Baptism*. Trans. and ed. Ernest Evans. London: SPCK, 1964.

_____. *Latin Christianity: Its Founder Tertullian*. Ed. Alexander Roberts and James Donaldson. Vol. 3: Ante-Nicene Fathers. New York: Charles Scribner's Sons, 1926.

_____. *Treatise on Penance*. Trans. William P. LeSaint. Vol. 28: Ancient Christian Writers. Westminster: Newman, 1959.

The Passion of the Scillitan Martyrs. Trans. Andrew Rutherford. Vol. 10: Ante-Nicene Fathers. New York: Charles Scribners Sons, 1926.

Theodore of Mopsuestia. *Commentary of Theodore of Mopsuestia on the Lord's Prayer and on the Sacraments of Baptism and the Eucharist*. Ed. A. Mingana. Vol. 6: Woodbrooke Studies. Cambridge: Heffer and Sons, 1933.

_____. *Commentary of Theodore of Mopsuestia on the Nicene Creed*. Ed. A. Mingana. Vol. 5: Woodbrooke Studies. Cambridge: Heffer and Sons, 1932.

Secondary Sources—Books

A Call to Action: An Agenda for the Catholic Community. Washington: United States Catholic Conference, 1977.

Aland, Kurt. *Did the Early Church Baptize Infants?* Trans. G. R. Beasley-Murray. Philadelphia: Westminster Press, 1963.

Austin, Gerard. *The Rite of Confirmation: Anointing with the Spirit*. New York: Pueblo, 1985.

Avila, Rafael. *Worship and Politics*. Maryknoll: Orbis, 1981.

Balasuriya, Tissa. *The Eucharist and Human Liberation*. Maryknoll: Orbis, 1979.

Barnes, Timothy David. *Tertullian: A Historical and Literary Study*. London: Oxford, 1971.

Barth, Karl. *The Teaching of the Church Regarding Baptism*. Trans. E. Payne. London: SCM Press, 1948.

Bauer, W. *Orthodoxy and Heresy in Earliest Christianity*. Philadelphia: Fortress, 1971.

Baumstark, A. *Comparative Liturgy*. Trans. F. Cross. Westminster: Newman Press, 1957.

Baur, Chrysostomus. *John Chrysostom and His Time*. Trans. S. M. Gonzaga. Westminster: Newman Press, 1959.

Beasley-Murray, George Raymond. *Baptism in the New Testament*. London: Macmillan, 1962.

_____. *Baptism and Today and Tomorrow*. New York: St. Martin's Press, 1966.

Benson, E. W. *Cyprian: His Life, His Times, His Work*. New York: Macmillan, 1897.

Bernier, Paul. *Bread Broken and Shared: Broadening Our Vision of the Eucharist*. Notre Dame: Ave Maria Press, 1981.

Boak, Arthur. *A History of Rome to 565 A.D.* New York: Macmillan, 1954.

Botte, Bernard. *From Silence to Participation: An Insider's View of Liturgical Renewal*. Trans. John Sullivan. Washington: Pastoral Press, 1988.

Bouyer, Louis. *Rite and Man*. Trans. M. Joseph Costelloe. Notre Dame: University of Notre Dame Press, 1963.

Brand, Eugene. *Baptism: A Pastoral Perspective*. Minneapolis: Augsburg, 1975.

Braxton, Edward K. *The Wisdom Community*. New York: Paulist Press, 1980.

Brett, Laurence. *Redeemed Creation*. Wilmington: Michael Glazier, 1984.

Buckley, Francis J. *"I Confess": The Sacrament of Penance Today*. Notre Dame: Ave Maria Press, 1972.

Cargas, Harry James and Bernard Lee, eds. *Religious Experience and Process Theology: The Pastoral Implications of a Major Modern Movement*. New York: Paulist Press, 1976.

Castelot, John J. *Anointing in the Old Testament*. Washington: Catholic University of America, 1950.

Chilson, Richard W. *A Lenten Pilgrimage—Dying and Rising in the Lord*. New York: Paulist Press, 1983.

Chittister, Joan D., and Martin, Marty, eds. *Faith and Ferment: An Interdisciplinary Study of Christian Beliefs and Practices*. Minneapolis: Augsburg, 1983.

Chrystal, James. *A History of the Modes of Christian Baptism*. Philadelphia: Lindsay & Blackeston, 1861.

Cote, Walfred Nelson. *The Archaeology of Baptism*. London: Yates & Alexander, 1876.

Cousins, Ewert, ed. *Process Theology*. New York: Newman, 1971.

Crehan, Joseph. *Early Christian Baptism and the Creed: A Study in Ante-Nicene Theology*. Westminster: Newman, 1950.

Crichton, J.D.C. *Christian Celebration: The Sacraments*. London: Geoffrey Chapman, 1973.

Crosby, Michael. *Spirituality of the Beatitudes: Matthew's Challenge for First-World Christians*. Maryknoll: Orbis, 1981.

Cullmann, Oscar. *Baptism in the New Testament*. Trans. J.K.S. Reid. Vol. 1: Studies in Biblical Theology. London: SCM Press, 1950.

Danielou, Jean. *L'Entrée dans L'Histoire du Salut.* Paris: Editions du Cerf, 1967.

Danielou, Jean, and Marrou, Henry. *The First Six Hundred Years.* Trans. Vincent Cronon. Vol. 1: The Christian Centuries. London: Darton, Longman, and Todd, 1964.

Davis, Charles. *The Making of a Christian: Five Lectures on Christian Initiation.* London: Sheed & Ward, 1964.

Devreesse, Robert. *Le Patriarchat d'Antioche depuis la paix de l'eglise jusqu'à la conquete Arabe.* Paris: Libraire Lecoffre, 1945.

Dix, Gregory. *The Shape of the Liturgy.* London: Dacre Press, 1945.

―――――. *The Theology of Confirmation in Relation to Baptism.* London: Dacre Press, 1946.

Dodds, E. R. *Pagan and Christian in an Age of Anxiety: Some Aspects of Religious Experience from Marcus Aurelius to Constantine.* Cambridge: Cambridge University Press, 1961.

Downey, Glanville. *A History of Antioch in Syria from Seleucus to the Arab Conquest.* Princeton: Princeton University Press, 1961.

―――――. *Ancient Antioch.* Princeton: Princeton University Press, 1963.

―――――. *Antioch in the Age of Theodosius the Great.* Norman: University of Oklahoma Press, 1962.

Duchesne, Louis. *Christian Worship: Its Origin and Evolution.* London: SPCK, 1903.

―――――. *Early History of the Christian Church from Its Foundation to the End of the Third Century.* New York: Longman & Green, 1909–24.

Duggan, Robert, ed. *Conversion and the Catechumenate.* New York: Paulist Press, 1984.

―――――. *Conversion in the ORDO INITIATIONIS CHRISTIANAE ADULTORUM: Analysis and Critique.* Ph.D. dissertation. Catholic University of America, 1980.

Dujarier, Michel. *A History of the Catechumenate: The First Six Centuries.* Trans. Edward J. Haasl. New York: Sadlier, 1979.

―――――. *Le Parrainage des adultes aux trois premiers siècles de l'Église: Recherche historique sur l'evolution des garanties et des étapes catéchuménales avant 313.* Paris: Editions du Cerf, 1962.

―――――. *The Rites of Christian Initiation: Historical and Pastoral Reflections.* Trans. and ed. Kevin Hart. New York: Sadlier, 1979.

Eisenhofer, Ludwig, and Lechner, Joseph. *The Liturgy of the Roman Rite.* Trans. A. J. and E. F. Peeler. New York: Herder and Herder, 1961.

Eliade, Mircea. *Patterns in Comparative Religion.* New York: Sheed and Ward, 1958.

Ellwood, Robert S. *Religious and Spiritual Groups in Modern America.* Englewood Cliffs: Prentice-Hall, 1973.

Ermoni, V. *Le Baptême dans l'église primitive.* Paris: Bloud & Cie, 1908.

Farnbridge, Maurice. *Studies in Biblical and Semitic Symbolism.* New York: Ktav, 1970.

Favazza, Joseph A. *The Order of Penitents: Historical Roots and Pastoral Future.* Collegeville: Liturgical Press, 1988.

Finn, Thomas M. *The Liturgy of Baptism in the Baptismal Instructions of St. John Chrysostom.* Washington: Catholic University of America Press, 1967.

Fisher, J.D.C. *Christian Initiation: Baptism in the Medieval West*. London: SPCK, 1965.

_____. *Christian Initiation: The Reformation Period*. London: SPCK, 1970.

_____. *Confirmation Then and Now*. London: SPCK, 1978.

_____. *The Fullness of Christian Initiation*. Oxford: Cowley, 1976.

Fredouille, Jean-Claude. *Tertullien et la conversion de la culture antique*. Paris: Etudes Augustiniennes, 1972.

Ganoczy, Alexander. *On Becoming Christian: A Theology of Baptism as the Sacrament of Human History*. Trans. John G. Lynch. New York: Paulist Press, 1976.

Gavin, F. *The Jewish Antecedents of the Christian Sacraments*. New York: Ktav, 1969.

George, Augustin. *Baptism in the New Testament*. Baltimore: Helicon, 1964.

Gilmore, Alex, ed. *Christian Baptism: A Fresh Attempt to Understand the Rite in Terms of Scripture, History and Theology*. Chicago: Judson, 1959.

Grant, Robert M. *Early Christianity and Society*. San Francisco: Harper and Row, 1977.

Greeley, Andrew. *Crisis in the Church: A Study of Religion in America*. Chicago: Thomas More Press, 1976.

_____. *The American Catholic: A Social Portrait*. New York: Basic Books, 1977.

Greer, Rowan. *Theodore of Mopsuestia: Exegete and Theologian*. London: The Faith Press, 1961.

Gremillion, J., and Castelli, J. *The Emerging Parish: The Notre Dame Study of Catholic Life since Vatican II*. San Francisco: Harper and Row, 1987.

Gula, Richard. *To Walk Together Again: The Sacrament of Reconciliation*. New York: Paulist Press, 1984.

Gusmer, Charles. *And You Visited Me: Sacramental Ministry to the Sick and Dying*. New York: Pueblo, 1984.

Gutierrez, Gustavo. *A Theology of Liberation: History, Politics and Salvation*. Trans. and ed. Sr. Caridad Inda and John Eagleson. Maryknoll: Orbis, 1973.

Hamman, Adalbert. *Le Baptême: faut-il baptiser aujourd'hui?* Paris: Editions du Cerf, 1971.

Harnak, Adolf. *History of Dogma*. Trans. Neil Buchanan. New York: Dover, 1961.

_____. *The Mission and Expansion of Christianity in the First Three Centuries*. Trans. J. Moffett. New York: Harper and Row, 1961.

Hegele, L. *Catechese mystagogique du baptéme*. Bruges: Abbaye de Saint-Andre, 1960.

Hertling, Ludwig. *COMMUNIO: Church and Papacy in Early Christianity*. Trans. Jared Wicks. Chicago: Loyola University Press, 1972.

Hesburgh, Theodore. *The Relation of the Sacramental Characters of Baptism and Confirmation to the Lay Apostolate*. Washington: Catholic University of America Press, 1948.

Holmes, Urban T. *Confirmation: The Celebration of Maturity in Christ*. New York: Seabury, 1975.

Howard, James Keir. *New Testament Baptism*. London: Pickering and Inglis, 1970.

Huels, John. *Disputed Questions in the Liturgy Today*. Chicago: Liturgy Training Publications, 1988.

Jeremias, Joachim. *Infant Baptism in the First Four Centuries*. Trans. David Cairns. Philadelphia: Westminster Press, 1962.

_____. *The Origins of Infant Baptism*. Trans. Dorothea M. Barton. Vol. 1: Studies in Historical Theology. London: SCM Press, 1963.

Jones, A.H.M. *Constantine and the Conversion of Europe*. Toronto: University of Toronto Press, 1979.

Kavanagh, Aidan. *Confirmation: Origins and Reform*. New York: Pueblo, 1988.

_____. *The Shape of Baptism: The Rite of Christian Initiation*. New York: Pueblo, 1978.

Kemp, Raymond B. *A Journey of Faith: An Experience of the Catechumenate*. New York: Sadlier, 1979.

Kennedy, Robert J., ed. *Reconciliation: The Continuing Agenda*. Collegeville: Liturgical Press, 1987.

Kidd, B. J. *A History of the Church to 461 A.D.* Oxford: Clarendon Press, 1922.

Kloppenburg, Bonaventure. *The Ecclesiology of Vatican II*. Trans. Matthew J. O'Connell. Chicago: Franciscan Herald Press, 1974.

Kubler-Ross, Elizabeth. *On Death and Dying*. New York: Macmillan, 1969.

Kung, Hans. *On Being a Christian*. Trans. Edward Quinn. Garden City: Doubleday, 1976.

_____. *Signposts for the Future: Contemporary Issues Facing the Church*. Garden City: Doubleday, 1978.

Lampe, Geoffrey William Hugo. *The Seal of the Spirit: A Study on the Doctrine of Baptism and Confirmation in the New Testament and the Fathers*. London: SPCK, 1967.

Laurentine, Andre, and Dujarier, Michel. *Catéchuménat, Données de l'histoire et perspectives nouvelles*. Paris: Editions du Centurion, 1969.

Lee, Bernard. *The Becoming of the Church: A Process Theology of the Structure of Christian Experience*. New York: Newman Press, 1974.

Lee, Bernard, gen. ed. *Alternative Futures for Worship*. 7 vols. Collegeville: Liturgical Press, 1987.

Leech, Kenneth. *Soul Friend*. San Francisco: Harper and Row, 1980.

Ligier, Louis. *La Confirmation: sens et conjuncture oecuménique hier et aujourd-'hui*. Paris: Beauchesne, 1973.

Lumpkin, William Latane. *A History of Immersion*. Nashville: Broadman, 1962.

McCormack, Arthur. *Christian Initiation*. New York: Hawthorne, 1969.

Maertens, Thierry. *Histoire et pastorale du rituel du catechumenat et du baptême*. Bruges: Biblica, 1962.

Manning, Frank. *A Call to Action: An Interpretative Summary and Guide*. Notre Dame: Fides, 1977.

Marsh, Thomas. *A Gift of Community: Baptism and Confirmation*. Wilmington: Michael Glazier, 1985.

Marstin, Ronald. *Beyond Our Tribal Gods: The Maturing Faith*. Maryknoll: Orbis, 1979.

Martos, Joseph. *Doors to the Sacred: A Historical Introduction to Sacraments in the Catholic Church*. Garden City: Doubleday, 1981.

Mick, Lawrence E. *RCIA: Renewing the Church as an Initiating Assembly*. Collegeville: Liturgical Press, 1989.

Mitchell, Leonel L. *Baptismal Anointing*. London: SPCK, 1966.

Mitchell, Nathan. *Mission and Ministry: History and Theology in the Sacrament of Order*. Wilmington, Michael Glazier, 1986.

Momigliano, Arnaldo, ed. *The Conflict between Paganism and Christianity in the Fourth Century*. Oxford: Clarendon, 1963.

Monceaux, Paul. *Histoire Litteraire de l'Afrique Chrétienne depuis les origines jusquá línvasion arabe*. Paris: Culture et Civilisation, 1901.

Moody, Dale. *Baptism: Foundation for Christian Unity*. Philadelphia: Westminster Press, 1967.

Morgan, James. *The Importance of Tertullian in the Development of Christian Dogma*. London: Kegan Paul, Trench, Trutner & Co., 1928.

Moss, Basil. *Crisis for Baptism: Report of the 1965 Ecumenical Conference Sponsored by the Parish and People Movement*. New York: Morehouse-Barlow, 1965.

Murphy Center for Liturgical Research, ed. *Made Not Born: New Perspectives on Christian Initiation and the Catechumenate*. Notre Dame: University of Notre Dame Press, 1976.

Naisbitt, John. *Megatrends: Ten New Directions Transforming Our Lives*. New York: Warner Books, 1984.

Neunheuser, Burkhard. *Baptism and Confirmation*. New York: Herder and Herder, 1964.

Parker, Henry Michael Denne. *A History of the Roman World 138–337*. Vol. 7: Methuen's History of the Greek and Roman World. London: Methuen, 1958.

Perry, Michael. *Crisis for Confirmation*. London: SCM Press, 1967.

Pocknee, Cyril Edward. *The Rites of Christian Initiation*. London: A. R. Mowbray, 1962.

Potel, J. *Moins de baptêmes en France. Pourquoi?* Paris: Editions du Cerf, 1974.

Power, David, M. and Maldonado, Luis, eds. *Liturgy and Human Passage*. Vol. 112: Concilium. New York: Seabury Press, 1979.

Rahner, Karl. *The Church and the Sacraments*. Trans. W. J. O'Hara. New York: Herder and Herder, 1963.

_____. *Theological Investigations III*. Baltimore: Helicon Press, 1968.

_____. *Theological Investigations VII*. London: Darton, Longman, and Todd, 1971.

Ratcliff, E. C. *Liturgical Studies*. Ed. A. H. Courain and D. H. Tripp. London: SPCK, 1976.

Reedy, William J., ed. *Becoming a Catholic Christian: A Symposium on Christian Initiation*. New York: Sadlier, 1979.

Reine, J. *The Eucharistic Doctrine and Liturgy of the Mystagogical Catecheses of Theodore of Mopsuestia*. Washington: Catholic University of America Press, 1942.

Riley, Hugh M. *The Rites of Christian Initiation of Adults: A Comparative Study of Interpretation of the Baptismal Liturgy in the Mystagogical Writings of St. Cyril of Jerusalem, St. John Chrysostom, Theodore of Mopsuestia and Ambrose of Milan*. Washington: Catholic University of America Press, 1974.

Sage, Michael. *Cyprian*. No. 1: Patristic Monograph Series. Cambridge, Mass.: The Philadelphia Patristic Foundation, 1975.

Schaff, Philip. *History of the Christian Church*. Grand Rapids: Eerdmans, 1910.

Schmeiser, James, ed. *Initiation Theology*. Toronto: Anglican Book Centre, 1978.

Shaughnessey, James D., ed. *The Roots of Ritual*. Grand Rapids: Eerdmans, 1973.

Sider, Robert Dick. *Ancient Rhetoric and the Art of Tertullian*. London: Oxford University Press, 1971.

Smith, Benjamin Franklin. *Christian Baptism: A Survey of Christian Teaching and Practice*. Nashville: Broadman Press, 1971.

Sontag, Susan. *AIDS and its Metaphors*. New York: Farrar, Straus and Giroux, 1989.

Sullivan, D. D. *The Life of the North Africans as Revealed in the Works of St. Cyprian*. Vol. 37: Patristic Studies. Washington: Catholic University of America Press, 1933.

Tillmans, Walter G., trans. *Confirmation: A Study Document Prepared by Commission on Education of the Lutheran World Federation*. Minneapolis: Augsburg, 1963.

Turner, Paul. *The Meaning and Practice of Confirmation: Perspectives from a Sixteenth-Century Controversy*. New York: Peter Lang, 1987.

Upton, Julia. *Journey into Mystery: A Companion to the RCIA*. New York: Paulist Press, 1986.

Vorgrimler, H. *Commentary on the Documents of Vatican II*. London: Herder, 1969.

Wagner, Johannes, ed. *Adult Baptism and the Catechumenate*. Vol. 22: Concilium. New York: Paulist Press, 1967.

Wainwright, Geoffrey. *Christian Initiation*. Richmond: John Knox Press, 1969.

Walker, G.S.M. *The Churchmanship of St. Cyprian*. Richmond: John Knox Press, 1968.

Wallis, Jim. *A Call to Conversion*. San Francisco: Harper and Row, 1981.

Warren, F. E. *The Liturgy and Ritual of the Ante-Nicene Church*. London: SPCK, 1912.

Warren, Michael. *Faith, Culture and the Worshiping Community*. New York: Paulist Press, 1989.

Whitaker, Edward Charles. *Documents of the Baptismal Liturgy*. London: SPCK, 1960.

_____. *Sacramental Initiation Complete in Baptism*. Bramcote: Grove Books, 1975.

White, Reginald. *The Biblical Doctrine of Initiation: A Theology of Baptism and Evangelization*. Grand Rapids: Eerdmans, 1960.

Wilde, James A., ed. *Before and After Baptism: The Work of Teachers and Catechists*. Chicago: Liturgy Training Publications, 1988.

_____. *Commentaries on the Rite of Christian Initiation of Adults*. Chicago: Liturgy Training Publications, 1988.

_____. *Finding and Forming Sponsors and Godparents*. Chicago: Liturgy Training Publications, 1988.

_____. *When Should We Confirm?* Chicago: Liturgy Training Publications, 1989.

Worgul, George S., Jr. *From Magic to Metaphor: A Validation of the Christian Sacraments*. New York: Paulist Press, 1980.

World Council of Churches. *One Lord, One Baptism: Study Report of the Faith and Order Commission.* London: SCM Press, 1961.

Yarnold, Edward. *The Awe-Inspiring Rites of Initiation: Baptismal Homilies of the Fourth Century.* Slough: St. Paul Publications, 1972.

Ysebaert, J. *Greek Baptismal Terminology: Its Origins and Early Development.* Nijmegen: Dekker & Van de Vegt, 1962.

Secondary Sources—Periodicals

Anderson, Herbert, and Foley, Edward. "Liturgy and Pastoral Care: The Parable of Dying and Grieving." *New Theology Review* 1/4 (November 1988) 15–28.

Armentraut, Donald S. "New Lutheran and Episcopal Baptismal Rites." *Lutheran Quarterly* 27 (1975) 295–311.

Arnett, Jean. "Development of an Adult Catechumenate in a Black Parish; Implications for the Church at Large." *Living Light* 15 (1978) 485–98.

Arrupe, Pedro. "The Hunger for Bread," *Address to the 41st International Eucharistic Congress.* Philadelphia, 1976.

Attenwiller, Bishop A. "Parish Renewal; a Process, Not a Program." *Origins* 8 (1979) 672–76.

Aubry, Andre. "Le projet pastoral du rituel de l'initiation des adultes." *Ephemerides Liturgicae* 88 (1974) 174–91.

Austin, Gerard. "The Essential Rite of Confirmation and Liturgical Tradition." *Ephemerides Liturgicae* 86 (1972) 214–24.

_____. "What Has Happened to Confirmation?" *Worship* 50 (1976) 420–26.

Baker, K. "A Guide to the 1974 Synod." *Homiletic and Pastoral Review* 75 (1975) 31–32.

Beckman, K. "L'initiation et la célébration baptismale dans les missions, du XVI siècle a nos jours." *La Maison-Dieu* 58 (1972) 48–70.

Beraudy, Roger. "Le nouveau rituel du baptême des adultes." *La Maison-Dieu* 121 (1975) 122–42.

_____. "Recherches theologiques autour du rituel baptismal des adultes." *La Maison-Dieu* 112 (1972) 25–50.

Bersten, John A. "Christian Affections and the Catechumenate." *Worship* 52 (1978) 194–210.

Bevenot, Maurice. "Cyprian's Platform in the Rebaptism Controversy." *Heythrop Journal* 19 (1978) 128–42.

"Beyond Religious Freedom: Church in Society." *Origins* 6 (1976) 404.

Bezzant, J. S. "Sin and Infant Baptism." *Theology* 62 (1959) 452.

Bonnard, Jean-Philippe. "Le temps du bapême: vers un catechumenat des enfants?" *Etudes* 333 (1970) 431–42.

Bourchard, C. "Journey of Faith: Initial Religious Formation as an Extension of the New Rite of Initiation of Adults." *Review for Religious* 36 (1977) 592–99.

Brand, Eugene L. "Baptism and Communion of Infants: A Lutheran View." *Worship* 50 (1976) 29–42.

Brimelow, T. "Confirmation: The Forgotten Sacrament." *Clergy Review* 60 (1975) 147–51.

Brusselmans, Christiane. "Christian Parents and Infant Baptism." *Louvain Studies* 2 (1968) 29–48.

Bryce, Mary Charles. "Confirmation: Being and Becoming Christian." *Worship* 41 (1967) 284–98.

Buckley, F. "The Right to the Sacraments of Initiation: The Individual and Community." *Origins* 8 (1978) 329–36.

_____. "What Age for Confirmation?" *Theological Studies* 27 (1966) 655–66.

Burghardt, Walter. "Catechetics in the Early Church: Program and Psychology." *Living Light* 1 (1964) 100–18.

Buswell, C. "Pastoral Suggestions for the Celebration of Confirmation." *Worship* 46 (1972) 30–34.

Butler, B. C. "St. Cyprian on the Church." *Downside Review* 71 (1952–53) 1–13; 119–34; 258–72.

Capelle, B. "L'introduction du catéchuménat á Rome au début de IIIe siécle." *Recherches de theologie ancienne et medieval* 5 (1933) 129–54.

Carter, R. "The Chronology of St. John Chrysostom's Early Life." *Traditio* 18 (1962) 359–64.

Cellier, Jacques. "Catéchuménes et communauté chrétienne." *La Maison-Dieu* 71 (1962) 142–51.

_____. "Le nouveau rite de l'initiation chrétienne des adultes." *Documentation Catholique* 69 (1972) 217–21.

Clarke, G.W. "Some Observations on the Persecution of Decius." *Antichthon* 3 (1969) 63–76.

_____. "The Barbarian Disturbances in North Africa of the Mid-Third Century." *Antichthon* 4 (1970) 78–84.

_____. "The Epistles of Cyprian." *Auckland Classical Essays Presented to E. M. Blaiklock.* (Oxford, 1970).

Clymer, Wayne K. "Pastoral Care and Infant Baptism." *Pastoral Psychology* 14 (1963) 31–36.

Congar, Yves. "Renewed Actuality of the Holy Spirit." *Lumen Vitae* 28 (1973) 13–31.

Coudreau, F. "The Catechumenate in France." *Worship* 42 (1968) 223–42.

Covino, Paul F. X. "The Postconciliar Infant Baptism Debate in the American Catholic Church." *Worship* 56 (1982) 240–60.

Crawford, Charles. "Infant Communion: Past Tradition and Present Practice." *Theological Studies* 31 (1970) 523–36.

Crehan, J. "Ten Years' Work on Baptism and Confirmation, 1945–1955." *Theological Studies* 17 (1956) 494–515.

Croix, G.E.M. de Ste. "Aspects of the 'Great' Persecution." *Harvard Theological Review* 47 (1954) 75–109.

Cude, Stephen D. "The Barth-Cullman Debate: Baptism in the New Testament." *Resonance* 6 (1968) 9–48.

Cunningham, Joseph L. "Confirmation: Pastoral Letdown." *America* 136 (1977) 164–66.

Daly, C. B. "Liturgical Worship in Tertullian's Africa." *Irish Ecclesiastical Record* 94 (1960) 136–46.

Dearden, John Cardinal. "Awakening a New Vision." *Origins* 4 (1975) 548.

Delcuve, Georges. "Becoming Christians in Christ: The Dynamics of the Sacraments of Baptism, Confirmation and Eucharist." *Lumen Vitae* 28 (1973) 77–97.

D'Ercole, Guiseppe. "The Presbyteral Colleges in the Early Church." *Concilium* 7 (1966) 12–18.

"Documents sur la confirmation." *Documentation Catholique* 68 (1971) 367–70.

Downey, Glanville. "Libanius' 'Oration in Praise of Ancient Antioch': Translation and Commentary." *Proceedings of the American Philosophical Society* 103 (1959) 652–86.

Dujarier, Michel. "Le catéchuménat et la maternité de l'Église." *La Maison-Dieu* 71 (1962) 78–94.

Dunning, James E. "Don't Dismiss the Dismissal: But Change the Name." *Church* 5/2 (Summer 1989) 34–37.

————. "The Rite of Christian Initiation of Adults: Model of Adult Growth." *Worship* 53 (1979) 142–57.

Erling, B. "Rites of Christian Initiation." *Lutheran Quarterly* 25 (1973) 254–69.

Finn, T. "Baptismal Death and Resurrection: A Study in Fourth-Century Eastern Baptismal Terminology." *Worship* 43 (1969) 175–89.

Fischer, Balthasar. "Baptismal Exorcism in the Catholic Baptismal Rites after Vatican II." *Studia Luturgica* 10 (1974) 48–55.

Ford, J. M. "Was Montanism a Jewish-Christian Heresy?" *Journal of Ecclesiastical History* 17 (1966) 145–58.

Fossion, Andre. "The Eucharist as an Act of Exchange." *Lumen* 35 (1980) 409–16.

Freeman, Grenville. "The Date of the Outbreak of Montanism." *Journal of Ecclesiastical History* 5 (1954) 7–15.

Garvey, Edwin. "Process Theology and the Crisis in Catechetics." *Homiletic and Pastoral Review* 74 (July 1974) 6–17.

Gilbert, John R. "The Reconciliation Service: A Reflection on Pastoral Experience as a Theological Source." *Worship* 59 (1985) 59–65.

Glaser, John W. "Conscience and Super-ego: A Key Distinction." *Theological Studies* 32 (1971) 30–47.

Granfield, Patrick. "Consilium and Consensus: Decision-Making in Cyprian." *Jurist* 35 (1975) 397–408.

Green, H. "The Significance of the Pre-Baptismal Seal in St. John Chrysostom." *Studia Patristica* 6 (1962) 84–90.

Gryson, R. "Les elections ecclesiastiques au IIIe siècle." *Revue d'Histoire Ecclesiastique* 68 (1973) 353–404.

Guerrette, Richard H. "Ecclesiology and Infant Baptism." *Worship* 44 (1970) 433–37.

Guillard, B. "Les étapes pastorales du catéchuménat." *La Maison-Dieu* 71 (1962) 131–42.

Gusmer, Charles. "Healing: Charism and Sacrament." *Church* 2 (1986) 16–22.

————. "The Revised Adult Initiation and Its Challenge to Religious Education." *Living Light* 13 (1973) 92–98.

Guyot, L. "Le sacrement de confirmation et les chrétiens d'aujourd'hui; pastoral letter." *Documentation Catholique* 68 (1971) 370–76.

Gwinnell, Michael. "The Age of Stage, for Confirmation." *Clergy Review* 55 (1970) 10–26.

Gy, Pierre-Marie. "Histoire liturgique de sacrement de confirmation." *La Maison-Dieu* 58 (1959) 135–45.

_____. "Le nouveau rite du baptême des adultes." *La Maison-Dieu* 71 (1962) 15–28.

_____. "Qu'est-ce qu'un catéchuméne?" *La Maison-Dieu* 71 (1962) 28–32.

_____. "The Idea of 'Christian Initiation.'" *Studia Liturgica* 12 (1977) 172–75.

_____. "Un document de la congregation pour la doctrine de la foi sur le baptême des petits enfants." *La Maison-Dieu* 104 (1970) 41–45.

Haggerty, Brian. "Toward a Catechesis of Confirmation." *Louvian Studies* 2 (1969) 334–54.

Harkins, P. W. "Pre-Baptismal Rites in Chrysostom's Baptismal Catechesis." *Studia Patristica* 8 (1963) 219–38.

Hiltner, S. "Minister and Process Theology." *Theology Today* 31 (1974) 99–103.

Holstein, Henri. "Le Baptême des petits enfants." *Etudes* 324 (1966) 547–51.

Honigmann, E. "The Patriarchate of Antioch." *Traditio* 5 (1947) 135–61.

Hubbard, Bishop H. "Shared Responsibility in the Local Church." *Origins* 11 (1979) 615–24.

Ivory, Thomas P. "The Restoration of the Catechumenate as a Norm for Catechesis." *Living Light* 13 (1976) 225–35.

_____. "The View from Senanque: The RCIA in International Perspective." *Living Light* 15 (1978) 469–75.

Jagger, Peter J. "The Anglican Rite of Infant Baptism: A Decade of Revision." *Worship* 45 (1971) 22–36.

Jenson, Robert. "On Infant Baptism." *Dialog* 8 (1960) 214–17.

_____. "The Eucharist: for Infants?" *Living Worship* 15/6 (June–July 1979).

Jugie, M. "Le *Liber ad Baptizandos* de Theodore de Mopsueste." *Echoes d'Orient* 34 (1935) 257–71.

Jungmann, Josef. "Liturgy, Devotions, and the Bishop." *Concilium* 2 (February 1965) 27–31.

Kavanagh, Aidan. "Adult Initiation: Process and Ritual." *Liturgy* 22/1 (1977) 5–10.

_____. "Christian Initiation for Those Baptized as Infants." *Living Light* 13 (1976) 387–96.

_____. "Christian Initiation in Post-Conciliar Roman Catholicism: A Brief Report." *Studia Liturgica* 12 (1977) 107–15.

_____. "Christian Initiation of Adults: The Rites." *Worship* 48 (1974) 318–35.

_____. "Confirmation: A Suggestion from Structure." *Worship* 58 (1984) 386–95.

_____. "Initiation." *Liturgy* 18/7 (1973) 4–8.

_____. "Initiation: Baptism and Confirmation." *Worship* 46 (1972) 262–76.

_____. "Liturgical Business Unfinished and Unbegun." *Worship* 50 (1976) 354–64.

_____. "Liturgical Needs for Today and Tomorrow." *Worship* 43 (1969) 488–95.

_____. "Recent Research on Christian Initiation." *Studia Liturgica* 12 (1967) 87–103.

_____. "The New Roman Rites of Adult Initiation." *Studia Liturgica* 10 (1974) 143–52.

_____. "The Norm of Baptism: The New Rite of Initiation of Adults." *Worship* 48 (1974) 143–52.

_____. "Unfinished and Unbegun Revisited: The Rite of Christian Initiation of Adults." *Worship* 53 (1979) 327–40.

_____. "What is Participation?" *Doctrine and Life* 23 (1973) 343–53.

Keating, Charles. "Baptism Sets Our Limits." *New Catholic World* 217 (1974) 100–104.

Keifer, Ralph. "Christian Initiation: The State of the Question." *Worship* 48 (1974) 392–404.

_____. "Confirmation and Christian Maturity: The Deeper Issue." *Worship* 46 (1972) 601–8.

Kemp, Raymond. "The Rite of Christian Initiation of Adults at Ten Years." *Worship* 56 (1982) 309–27.

Kiesling, Christopher. "Infant Baptism." *Worship* 42 (1968) 617–26.

Kilian, Sabbas. "Mission of the Church: To Humanize or Divinize." *Proceedings of the Catholic Theological Society of America* 31 (1976).

Kucera, Archbishop. "Liturgy and the Sacraments." *Origins* 18 (March 23, 1989) 695–96.

Kung, Hans. "Confirmation: What's the Fuss?" *U.S. Catholic* 40 (July 1975) 19–22.

Lanne, Emmanuel. "Église locales et patriarchats á l'epoque de grands conciles." *Irenikon* 34 (1961) 292–321.

Larson, Jan R. "Age and Confirmation." *Modern Liturgy* 6 (March–April 1979) 6–8.

Laurentin, A. "A propos du rituel du baptême des adultes." *Paroisse et liturgie* 44 (1962) 230–38.

"Le nouveau rituel de la confirmation." *Documentation Catholique* 68 (1971) 855–56.

Lebreton, J. "Les Origines du symbole baptismal." *Recherches de Science Religieuse* 20 (1930) 97–124.

Lemming, Bernard. "On the Theology of Infant Baptism." *Heythrop Journal* 4 (1963) 386–92.

Lesousky, A. "Traditional Thought Processes in Saint Cyprian's Letters." *Classical Bulletin* 33 (1956) 16–17.

Liege, A. "Le baptême des enfants dans le débat pastoral et theologique." *La Maison-Dieu* 107 (1971) 7–28.

Ling, Richard. "A Cathechist's Vote for Infant Confirmation." *Living Light* 7 (1970) 42–56.

Lottus, J. "Vatican II's Model of the Church." *New Blackfriars* 59 (1978) 392–401.

McKenzie, John L. "A New Study of Theodore of Mopsuestia." *Theological Studies* 10 (1949) 394–408.

McKeon, Michael. "Confirmation Past and Present." *Modern Liturgy* 6 (March–April 1979) 4–5.

McManus, Frederick. "Adult Baptism." *Worship* 37 (1963) 257–59.

_____. "The Restored Liturgical Catechumenate." *Worship* 36 (1962) 536–49.

McNamara, Kevin. "The Fourth Synod of Bishops." *Furrow* 26 (1975) 5–24.

Mainelli, Eugene A. "The Parish Community Becoming: Theological Reflections." *Social Thought* 1 (Fall 1975) 11–27.

Mannion, M. Francis. "Penance and Reconciliation: A Systemic Analysis." *Worship* 60 (1986) 98–119.

Marcus, Emile. "Qui doit-on laisser accéder aux sacrements?" *Paroisse et Liturgie* 46 (1964) 497–516.

Marsh, T. "A Study of Confirmation." *Irish Theological Quarterly* 39 (1972) 149–63; 319–35; 40 (1973) 125–47.

_____. "Confirmation and Its Relation to Baptism." *Irish Theological Quarterly* 27 (1960) 259–93.

_____. "The History and Significance of the Post-Baptismal Rites." *Irish Theological Quarterly* 29 (1962) 175–206.

_____. "The Theology of Confirmation." *Furrow* 27 (1976) 606–16.

Miller, Randolph C. "Process Thinking and Religious Education." *Anglican Theological Review* 57 (1975) 271–88.

Mitchell, Leonel. "The Baptismal Rite in Chrysostom." *Anglican Theological Review* 43 (1961) 397–403.

_____. "Revision of the Rites of Christian Initiation in the American Episcopal Church." *Studia Liturgica* 10 (1974) 25–34.

Mitchell, Nathan. "The Adult Catechumenate in an Age of Pluralism." *Liturgy* 22/1 (1977) 11–17.

Moingt, Joseph. "L'initiation chrétienne des jeunes." *Etudes* 336 (1972) 599–617.

Molin, Jean-Baptiste. "Le nouvel rituel de l'initiation chrétienne des adultes." *Notitae* 8 (1972) 87–95.

Nocent, Adrian. "Confirmation: The Difficult Catechesis." *Lumen Vitae* 28 (1973) 97–113.

O'Connell, B. "The New Rite of Adult Baptism." *Clergy Review* 48 (1963) 352–62.

Orianne, J. "Baptism." *Lumen Vitae* 26 (1971) 623–48.

Paliard, Charles. "La conversion et les étapes dans le catéchuménat." *La Maison-Dieu* 71 (1962) 94–131.

Parker, J. "The Adult Catechumenate: Pastoral Suggestions for Lent." *Living Light* 15 (1978) 476–84.

Payne, Ernest A. "Baptism and Christian Initiation." *Baptist Quarterly* 26 (1975) 147–57.

"Personhood: Justice Conference Resolutions." *Origins* 6 (1976).

Philibert, Paul. "Children's Ritual Enculturation: What, How and Why?" *Catechumenate* 11 (March 1989) 27–44.

Piana G. "The Roman Church at the End of the Second Century." *Harvard Theological Review* 18 (1925) 201–77.

Pocknee, C.E. "Confirmation and the Reconciliation of Heretics and Apostates." *Church Quarterly Review* 166 (1963) 357–61.

Porter, H. Boone. "Baptism: Its Paschal and Ecumenical Setting." *Worship* 42 (1968) 205–14.

Power, David. "Let the Sick Man Call." *Heythrop Journal* 19 (1978) 256–70.

Power, Kathryn. "Adult Catechumenate and Confirmation." *Modern Liturgy* 6 (March–April 1979) 28–30.

Powers, Joseph "Confirmation: The Problem of Meaning." *Worship* 46 (1972) 22–29.

Quasten, Johannes. "The Blessing of the Baptismal Font in the Syrian Rite of the Fourth Century." *Theological Studies* 7 (1946) 309–13.

Ratzinger, Joseph. "Taufe, Glaube und Zeigshorigkeit zur Kirche." *Communio* 5 (1976) 218–34.

Redmond, Richard X. "Infant Baptism: History and Pastoral Problems." *Theological Studies* 30 (1969) 79–89.

Reichert, R. "A Catechist's Response to the Rite of Christian Initiation for Adults." *Living Light* 14 (1977) 138–46.

Reinhard, P. "Note sur la nécessité pastorale d'un d'accuil des enfants au Nord-Togo." *La Maison-Dieu* 98 (1969) 59–62.

Renoux, A. "L'ancien rituel romain du catéchuménat et notre Ordo du baptême des adults." *La Maison-Dieu* 71 (1962) 32–46.

Rey, Bernard. "L'Église et la baptême des enfants." *Revue des sciences philosophiques et theologiques* 52 (1968) 677–97.

Roberto, John. "Giving Direction to Confirmation." *Living Worship* 15 (May 1979).

Rusling, G. W. "The Status of Children." *Baptist Quarterly* 18 (1959–60) 245–57.

Ryan, L. "Patristic Teaching on the Priesthood of the Faithful." *Irish Theological Quarterly* 29 (1962) 25–57.

Ryder, A. "Parents' Faith and Infant Baptism." *Clergy Review* 58 (1973) 746–59.

Sawicki, Marianne. "The Process of Consensus: Purpose, Papers and Proceedings of the Synod." *Living Light* 15 (1978) 7–31.

Senn, Frank C. "New Baptismal Rite: Toward Revitalizing the Whole Community." *Currents in Theology and Mission* 2 (1975) 206–14.

Shepherd, Massie. "Confirmation: The Early Church." *Worship* 46 (1972) 15–21.

Stephenson, A. "The Lenten Catechetical Syllabus in Fourth-Century Jerusalem." *Theological Studies* 15 (1954) 103–16.

Stevick, Daniel. "Confirmation for Today: Reflections on the Rite Proposed for the Episcopal Church." *Worship* 44 (1970) 541–60.

_____. "Types of Baptismal Spirituality." *Worship* 47 (1973) 11–26.

Talley, Thomas J. "Ordination in Today's Thinking." *Studia Liturgica* 13 (1979) 4–10.

Telfer, W. "The Origins of Christianity in Africa." *Studia Patristica* 4 (1961) 512–17.

"The Thirty-Four Points." *L'Osservatore Romano* (Eng) (November 17, 1977) 6–7; *Living Light* 15 (1978) 74–80.

Tietjen, M. "A Kingly People." *Living Light* 7 (1971) 119–21.

"Toward a Neo-Catechumenate: Synod Intervention of Cardinal Leo Suenens." *Origins* 7 (1977) 296–98.

Tozzi, E. "Confirmation: Clarifying the Choices." *Living Light* 11 (1974) 549–62.

Turner, Victor. "Passages, Margins, and Poverty: Religious Symbols of Communitas." *Worship* 46 (1972) 390–412, 482–94.

Upton, Julia Ann. "A Solution to the Infant Baptism Problem." *Living Light* 16 (1979) 484–96.

Vanbergen, Paul. "Baptism of the Infants of *non satiscredentes* Parents." *Studia Liturgica* 12 (1977) 195–200.

Wainwright, G. "Baptismal Eucharist before Nicea: An Essay in Liturgical History." *Studia Liturgica* 4 (1965) 9–36.

_____. "Développements baptismaux depuis 1967." *Etudes Theologiques et Religieuses* 49 (1974) 67–93.

_____. "The Rites and Ceremonies of Christian Initiation." *Studia Liturgica* 10 (1974) 2–24.

Watson, Dorothy. "Confirmation and the Adolescent." *Furrow* 21 (1970) 212–47.

Webb, Dom Bruno. "Unbaptized Infants and the Quasi-Sacrament of Death." *Downside Review* 71 (1952–53) 243–57.

Weil, Louis. "Christian Initiation: A Theological and Pastoral Commentary on the Proposed Rites." *Saint Luke's Journal of Theology* 18 (1975) 95–112.

Whitehead, J. and E., and Myers, G. "The Parish and Sacraments of Adulthood: Accesses to an Educational Future." *Listening* 12 (1977) 83–100.

Wiles, M. F. "The Theological Legacy of St. Cyprian." *Journal of Ecumenical History* 14 (1963) 139–49.

Worgul, G. "Is Confirmation the Real Problem?" *Religion Teacher's Journal* 10 (1977) 24–26.

_____. "The Ecclesiology of 'The Rite of Christian Initiation of Adults.'" *Louvain Studies* 6 (1976) 159–69.

Wright, John Cardinal. "Some Reflections on Confirmation." *L'Osservatore Romano* (Eng) (June 1, 1978) 9–10.

Yarnold, Edward. "Baptism and the Pagan Mysteries in the Fourth Century." *Heythrop Journal* 13 (1972) 247–67.

Zernov, N. "Saint Stephen and the Roman Community at the Time of the Baptismal Controversy." *Church Quarterly Review* 117 (1934) 304–36.

Ziegler, John J. "Who Can Anoint the Sick." *Worship* 61 (January 1987) 25–44.

Index